GW00854461

The
BUSINESS
VOYAGE

Secrets of Business Success and Fulfillment Revealed

Jonathan Blain

ASAP™
INSTITUTE

© 2005 Jonathan Blain. All rights reserved.

Published by ASAP Institute
Adventure House
91 Deanfield Road
Henley on Thames
Oxfordshire
RG9 1UU
UK

enquiry@asapinstitute.com
www.asapinstitute.com

To obtain your free audio message from the author, register at the following Web site: www.thebusinessvoyage.com/bv/buyerregistration.htm and enter the following serial number: BVED1FRMJB

Cartoons by Roy Nixon
Edited by Linda Hines
Cover and book designed by Andrea Jensen
Indexing by Samita Jana
Proofreading by David Hines
Edited in American English

Printed in Great Britain by Lightning Source
ISBN: 978-1-905243-00-6

Leaders of U.K. Top 1,000 Companies

"A great practical introduction to anyone interested in running their own business, but are not sure how to go about it."
— Charles Dunstone, CEO, Carphone Warehouse

"This book is full of insight and sound advice and should be a 'must read' for all aspiring business managers and entrepreneurs — or even those who just want to manage their personal lives better! Jonathan Blain explains in this book what took me 25 years to work out for myself. Read it now to get on the fast track to personal and business success."
— Nigel Gardener, MD Kingsland Wines and Spirits

"Thought-provoking ideas presented in refreshingly accessible language."
— Ruurd de Fluiter, Chief Executive Officer, Swiss Re UK Ltd.

"It does not matter if you are new to management or are a seasoned campaigner this book will give you food for thought, whether it's building effective teams or resetting your work life balance, there is something for everyone. This book made me think again on whether I was doing everything I could to be successful. You really are in control of your own destiny and this book makes you realise this in the nicest possible way.

An engaging book which personally helped me put some things into perspective, I know I'm in control of my own destiny, but this book helped put a nice framework on how I do something about it, both in work and my private life.

Lots of useful tools and tips to help anyone get more out of their business and private lives, easy to read and a great reality check for all of us."
— Mark Rogers, General Manager, Apple Computer (UK) Ltd.

"This is an excellent book that all managers and would-be managers should read carefully. There are parts that will have you desperate to call the author to debate his views and to show how things in your company are very different — other parts will make you very quiet and contemplative.

I particularly liked the thread that seemed to run through the book about 'attitude.' Jonathan Blain seems to share my view that if a person's attitude is right almost anything can be achieved."
— Steve Dowdle, Managing Director, Sony UK Sales Company

"This book is a wonderful example of 'Common Sense' and pragmatism."
— Tim Jolly, Chief Executive, Princes Foods Manufacturing Group

"A journey through this book is full of the right stuff for the budding Entrepreneur and ambitious Manager."
— John Rackstraw, Chief Executive, Pearce Group Ltd.

"Anyone who wants to realise their full potential in business and their personal life should read this book. It will act as an invaluable reference book and one of the best investments an individual could make in order to improve their journey through life."

— Michael Wilson, Chairman, St James's Place Wealth Management Group plc

"Very well written ... a good read. Expressed commonsense views and I'm sure will appeal to a wide cross section of both mature and upcoming businessmen."

— John Tong, Managing Director, Finnforest UK

Business Organizations

"An excellent new approach to business, some very interesting and enjoyable perspectives on business life."

— Miles Templeman, Director General, Institute of Directors

Military Organizations

"Professional standards, teamwork, ethos and the acceptance of real responsibility are the bedrock of military management. The Royal Navy has learnt much from the business world in the last 20 years, Jonathan Blain's sea-going experiences, backed up with a healthy dose of his military sense of humour, reveal some of the 'secrets' that have made the U.K. Armed Forces the best in the world today!"

— Admiral Sir Jonathon Band KCB, Royal Navy, First Sea Lord and Chief of Naval Staff

Directors of U.K. Medium-Sized Enterprises

"Jonathan Blain's book is a 'must read' for all studying MBAs — he transforms the meaning of MBA to 'Make Business Adventurous' ...

A voyage of discovery you must read and experience if you want to be a sensational success in business. Read it — Absorb it — then just DO IT."

— Dawn Gibbins, Chairman, Flowcrete Group plc

Directors of U.K. Small-Sized Enterprises

"The case studies really brought your thinking to life and had me captivated; your energy and enthusiasm for the adventure that is business inspired me."

— Steve Marshal, Founder of Reflexion Consulting Ltd.

"Jonathan Blain's 'Business Voyage' is quite simply an inspirational treasure chest. Every time you dip into it you find wonderful pearls of wisdom and golden nuggets of information.

It's a must-read for anyone starting their own business, growing an existing business, or simply thinking about changing their life.

Easy to read format, wonderful cartoons and friendly, down-to-earth approach makes it highly readable and accessible to everyone."
— Naomi Saunders, Founder, Clearly Organised

Entrepreneurs

"An ambitious, readable and engaging journey of entrepreneurial risk-taking. Jonathan is a master of defying odds and making things happen. This book will inspire you to challenge yourself and others to attempt the improbable and fail only the impossible."
— Gill Marer, Founder, All for Success

Comments on *The Business Voyage* at Motivation Show, Chicago, IL, 2004

"A unique approach to understanding and engaging the business voyage."
— Doug Seville, C Paths

"Very informative, a must read book."
— Lee Salberg, Lee Salberg Int. Group

"Jonathan breaks down ideas and presents suggestions in a clear and usable manner."
— J.T. Breslin, PMX Ind., Inc.

"A blueprint to obtaining and maintaining a successful business. Very informative and personable insights from Jonathan."
— Jerry Bourgois, Spectator Sport Specials

"Very interesting."
— Jack Mills

"One need look no further than his own home to realise the importance of a good foundation. Jonathan looks at every constructive aspect of building a successful business and enjoys it."
— Mick Long, Brandprokin International

"This book is going to be incredible for anyone thinking of owning their own business."
— Michael Skelton

"This book is not an ordinary business read, it is an extraordinary look at how life and business are partners."
— Cheryl Landman

Jonathan Blain would like to thank the following people for their best wishes and support.

	JOB TITLE	ORGANIZATION
Martin Sorrell	CEO	WPP
Arun Sarin	CEO	Vodafone
RD Peters	CEO	P&O Ferries
Philip Bowman	CEO	Allied Domecq
Rob Templeman	Chief Executive	Debenhams Retail
Philip Dearing	Chief Executive	Market Harborough Building Society
John McAdam	Chief Executive	ICI
Richard Baker	Chief Executive	Boots Group plc
Alberto Chiarini	Chief Executive	Eni UK Ltd.
Dave Gilbert	Managing Director	Waterstones
Peter Blackwell	Chairman and Managing Director	Kodak Ltd.
Jean-Pierre Garnier	Chief Executive	GlaxoSmithKline plc
Charles Allen	Chief Executive	ITV plc
Sir Stuart Hampson	Chairman	John Lewis Partnership
Graham Smith	Managing Director	Toyota (GB) plc
Sir Fred Goodwin	Group Chief Executive	The Royal Bank of Scotland Group plc
Alan Giles	Chief Executive	HMV Group plc
Brian Duffin	Chief Executive	Scottish Life
Alan Parker	Chief Executive	Whitbread plc
Peter Johnson	Group Executive	Inchcape plc
Iain Cornish	Chief Executive	Yorkshire Building Society
Joe Plumeri	Chairman and Chief Executive	Willis
Mark Thompson	Director General	BBC

The

BUSINESS
VOYAGE

Secrets of Business Success
and Fulfillment Revealed

Jonathan Blain

The business leader's voyage of discovery to
business success and personal fulfillment.
The real business world uncovered.

ABOUT THE AUTHOR

Jonathan Blain is an explorer, adventurer, and innovator in life and business. He is also a serial entrepreneur and leading business visionary. When it comes to taking on new challenges, both personal and business, Jonathan is at the front of the line. To Jonathan, taking risks means living life to the fullest. During his short career commission as a Royal Naval Officer, he became the youngest compliment officer in the fleet, survived a hurricane in the mid Atlantic, and narrowly missed being sunk on HMS Coventry during the Falklands war. His adventures continued in the Fishery Protection Squadron arresting fishing boats, responding to a fire on the Piper Alpha oil rig, and taking part in search and rescue operations. His personal life has been action-packed and adventure-filled. He survived in mountainous seas when his yacht started to break up in the North Atlantic during the Two-handed Transatlantic Yacht Race. He designed and skippered his yacht in the Governor's Cup Yacht Race, some 1,700 miles from Cape Town to the tiny and remote island of St. Helena in the South Atlantic. He has encountered guerrillas in the Philippines, an ambush in Thailand, and whales in the Bay of Biscay.

Ten exciting years with the Mobil Oil Corporation, then the world's fourth largest company, gave him a colorful insight into big corporate business in a variety of different roles. From the earliest age, entrepreneurship blossomed, but after leaving Mobil, Jonathan caught the entrepreneurship bug seriously. A massive variety of business experiences in a wide range of business sectors gave Jonathan a unique insight into the challenges facing business leaders. He is frank about his amazing highs and lows; he has made and lost £30 million. He pulled off a £500,000 joint venture with a top U.K. 100 company and floated twenty percent of his company for £5.4 million, a record IPO on the market. Jonathan also knows a thing or to about tight corners and tough business situations. He has a storybook of personal experiences as long as your arm, which reflects considerable, hands-on experience at the sharp end.

A realist with a positive outlook on life, Jonathan is an accomplished author with an International bestseller, Special Edition Using SAP R/3 and many other books to his name with sales of over $3.8 million. He is naturally inventive and creative and has emerged as an inspirational "thought leader" in the business world. Making sense of the exciting, chaotic, and confusing business world and life in general has led him to a number of interesting discoveries and highly practical solutions. Ever the explorer, he is on a continual quest to make new discoveries and to go where others have rarely gone before.

As well as being an author, business person and TV commentator, Jonathan is a Consultant – providing ideas and strategy to leading organisations, a Keynote Speaker at meetings, conferences and seminars, a Coach and Mentor to top business leaders and Non Executive Director of quoted and non-quoted companies.

AUTHOR'S ACKNOWLEDGEMENTS

I would like to thank everyone who has helped and supported me, in particular my family, especially my dear wife, Jennifer.

The following people have supported me in producing this book:

Kezia, Xanthe, and Talia, my adorable daughters, for their welcome interruptions

Julie Trent, whose loyalty and honesty has been invaluable

Sarah Fearn, who has lived through the ups and downs and kept the faith

Linda Hines and Andrea Jensen for their editorial and design expertise

Roy Nixon for his cartoons and Samita Jana for her indexing

David Hines for his proofreading

Simon McNeill-Ritchie for his moral support

Russell O'Connell, who has shared the same vision

Barry Rogers, who has helped unlock secrets

Fay Rutherford, Gillian McKinnon, and Mary West for their help in typing and offering advice

Kirti Dasani and Simon Sheehan for being good friends

John Hancock and Alun Davies for acting as a sounding board

John and Elaine Peck for their energy, enthusiasm, and support

Gil Marer for his encouragement

Les Green for his insight

Mark Wilson for helping when I needed help

Steve Dunning for providing promotional photography

Chris Cohen for his tremendous IT support

David Sales for his promotional support

Jon Johnston and Winston Squire for keeping me fit

Naomi Saunders for keeping the mountains of paper under control

Daphne Rotenberg and Mary Flavelle for lifting my spirits

Barney Green and Catherine Denning for their real-life stories

Nick Parkin for his extraordinary generosity

Andy Roberts for producing the promotional presentation materials

Rob Churchward for his professional help

All those who have been kindhearted in offering positive quotes, help, and advice

TABLE OF CONTENTS

THE BUSINESS VOYAGE
SECRETS OF BUSINESS SUCCESS AND FULFILLMENT REVEALED

PERSONAL MESSAGE FROM THE AUTHOR

When I graduated from school, I knew I wanted to be a businessman. My father always ran his own businesses, mostly in the clothing trade, importing women's apparel to the United Kingdom from around the world. Under his leadership, a U.K. closed-circuit television company grew to a significant size, so I believe business is in my blood. From an early age, I sold rose petal perfume in jam jars to neighbors, traded marbles and collector cards at primary school, then moved on to deal making and trading in secondary school. While still at school, I sold watches that I purchased from wholesalers on a consignment basis and managed to sell skateboard clothing to a large department store chain. One hot summer I decided it would be a good idea to sell milk to Japanese tourists who frequented a nearby park. That business was short-lived when local vendors, irritated by the fact I had attracted large crowds of customers, made sure I didn't return when they discovered I had no vendor's license.

Entrepreneurship has always intrigued me. When I see opportunities I feel compelled to seize them, and I frequently do. I have had experience running a wide variety of businesses, in different market segments — business to business (B2B), business to consumer (B2C), service, and manufacturing.

As well as running my own small businesses, I have worked for some of the largest. I have run a public limited company (PLC), limited companies, not-for-profit companies, and I have operated as a sole trader. I have managed lots of people, small teams, and operated as a one-man band.

Over the years there is not much I haven't experienced, from armed robberies to staff fraud and theft. Nothing surprises me, and I have learned that in business, like being at sea, you need to be prepared to cope with every eventuality. I have had almost as varied experiences at sea as I have had in business. I see a stream of analogies between the nautical and business worlds, hence the title The Business Voyage.

When I was just three years old, my parents noticed I was drawn to water and boats, a little unusual perhaps, considering I was brought up in Sutton Coldfield near Birmingham in the United Kingdom, which is about as far away from the sea as you can get. This connection with water and boats remains with me today and has been an important part of my life.

Throughout my childhood, I did everything I could to play with boats and water. I was in the Sea Cubs, Sea Scouts, and joined a local sailing club. On leaving school, I joined the Royal Navy as a Seaman Officer and became a professional seaman, gaining a "Bridge Watch-Keeping Certificate." Since that time I have owned a small flotilla of boats including five yachts, the last of which I had designed and custom built to my exact requirements. Nautical adventures have been an important part of my life. You learn a tremendous amount by stepping outside your comfort zone, embarking on adventures of any kind, and surviving on your knowledge, instincts, and skills.

After completing my Commission in the Royal Navy, I joined Mobil Oil Corporation, which was then the fourth largest company in the world, where I spent ten happy and interesting years. After leaving I spent nearly ten years working for myself, running a large number of different businesses. As a serious and committed entrepreneur, I have had my fair share of highs and lows, and I have learned many lessons, the most important of which is to never stop learning.

I started writing about business and technology in the mid nineties. My first book, Special Edition Using SAP R/3, an international bestseller, deals with business process re-engineering, the issues surrounding technology use in business, and SAP, a leading computer software system.

I have come to realize there are a lot of things they should teach at business school that they don't. I hope you find this book enjoyable, enlightening, informative, and thought provoking. You can read it from cover to cover or dip in and out as your interests dictate to find solutions or insights to the unique issues that you may be facing. This book is intended for everyone interested in business, whether you are a leader of a top-1000 company, a director, manager, business owner, entrepreneur, or someone looking to start your first business.

In this book you will find:

1. Concepts and ideas
2. Real-life stories and anecdotes including many from the author's varied and interesting life
3. Inspiring quotations
4. Words of Wisdom
5. Graphical illustrations

To help navigate your way through this book the following icons have been used:

 1. Decision Point

 4. Thought Starter

 2. Important Concept or Tip

 5. Warning

 3. Navigation Tool

FOREWORD

OBJECTIVE

Do you "live to work" or "work to live?" I suggest, for most people, the answer is a bit of both. Business success and personal fulfillment are inextricably linked. Most people have private and work lives. Of necessity, we need to work to earn money to afford our lifestyle, have a home to live in, clothes to wear, food to eat, etc. Even people who are seriously wealthy and arguably don't need to work to earn money, find they need to work to gain purpose and fulfillment in their lives. This is human nature.

WORK AND LIFE BALANCE

It is fairly common for the average person to work forty or more hours a week. In general, business leaders work considerably longer. During the working part of our lives, work time typically accounts for thirty-five percent of our waking time.

BUSINESS LEADER FRUSTRATIONS

Business leaders have the keys to business success, yet knowing how to unlock it can be intolerably frustrating and difficult. I know this from bitter personal experience. In this book you won't find all the answers, but you will find a route to success and a unique perspective on the business issues of today. As a business leader you must understand that it is you and only you who can travel the route. If you have this book in your hands and are reading this forward in a bookstore, or better still have already bought it, then the likelihood is you want to start your own personal voyage of self-discovery and quest for business success. Personal fulfillment and business success are relative concepts; it is for you to decide what yours look like.

WHY THIS BOOK IS DIFFERENT

For all the business concepts, knowledge, and training available worldwide, most businesses could do better and most struggle to achieve the success their leaders seek. Why, therefore, do I think I can help you achieve what others have not?

My answer lies in my approach, which is to give you an uplifting and visionary perspective on the practical issues you face and show you the routes to take. You will discover your own answers, explore new routes, and create new perspectives and make new discoveries.

Business schools teach a considerable amount about business. There are things all of us in business simply need to understand and they generally do a good job in helping us. In this book you will find some of the things they don't teach you, things learned through trial and error, in the school of hard knocks.

Reality and theory can often be very different; this book explains some of the reasons why. Gaining an understanding and seeing the truth will help you make sense of the often chaotic and sometimes unpredictable business world. The underlying concept throughout this book is "common sense" and helping you see things in a different way.

THE PATH TO BUSINESS SUCCESS
There is a multitude of different things that make businesses successful; if only it could be bottled, someone would make a fortune. The reality is that a number of factors join together in particular circumstances, which means that in different circumstances the same factors would not necessarily produce the same results.

Can you imagine the results if one of the giant global technology companies was a new company starting in business today, with the same people, same finances, resources, etc.? It is highly unlikely they could repeat their success because circumstances are different. Likewise, business leaders who have achieved extraordinary success in one business are not guaranteed to do the same in another, something investors find difficult to understand.

SUCCESSFUL LEADERS SHARE A COMMON THREAD
The common thread is not what you know; it is the unstoppable need to know more. If you look at most high-profile, successful entrepreneurs you will usually see that they have had their share of failures along the way, yet they persevere. Not every business works.

Have you ever felt that your business was like a partially inflated balloon, where you grasp one issue and another seems to appear somewhere else? You grasp that and another appears somewhere else again? This book explains why you might experience this phenomenon and shows you how to get your business and personal life under control, where they become more manageable, predictable, and enjoyable.

PREPARE TO START YOUR VOYAGE OF DISCOVERY

If you feel encouraged to start your voyage, be prepared to start thinking in new and innovative ways. This book addresses modern business territory; it explores routes to better self-understanding and the importance of balance between your work and private life. The voyage starts with this self-understanding. The next step is the business conception and foundation-building that is so important prior to commencing trade. It then goes through the business trials, tribulations, and triumphs, from the time of the first sale to the last. Finally, the knowledge and experience gathered along the way are condensed into a business blueprint you can use for your own voyage, and you are left with an alternative perspective on the fundamental business issues and indicators to guide you into the future.

....

WORDS OF WISDOM

Most high profile entrepreneurs have had failures along the way; business is full of risk and not everything will work.

The only things that are right are those which work.

....

INTRODUCTION

BUSINESS AS AN ADVENTURE

"Adventure is in the eye of the beholder; it is a relative concept that is personal to the individual." — Jonathan Blain

I have come to the conclusion that in much of the modern world, we have had adventure knocked out of us to the extent we lack ambitious goals and fear risk and uncertainty.

DEFINITION OF ADVENTURE

"An undertaking that involves risk and uncertainty in the hope of positive outcomes with the expectation of excitement."
— Jonathan Blain

In reality, life and business are both adventures, we simply tend not to see them as that. We need to learn to create ambitious goals and to manage risk and uncertainty.

THE ADVENTURE PROCESS

Process	Description
Think	*What, how, why*
Look	*When, where*
See	*Tune in and take in*
Understand	*Awareness and knowledge*
Act	*Do something*
Results	*Outcomes which can be positive, negative, or neutral*
Analyze	*Assess results of actions*

Continually repeat this process.

I am part of a trio of public speakers called "The Three Adventurers" comprised of John Peck, Paul Bennett, and me. Through different experiences we have come to realize the importance of adventure in lives and business. Adventure doesn't have to be climbing Mount Everest, sailing an ocean, or any such grand enterprise. It can be as simple as making a small improvement in business or life.

We believe we are all adventurers in life and business; we just don't see ourselves as such. The only certainty we have is that we and our businesses will eventually die; it is the how and when we don't know. Morbid thoughts, perhaps, but realizing the risk and uncertainty and dealing with them in a positive way can lead to incredible achievements.

Being an adventurer is about changing lives and personal and work outcomes. To be an adventurer you need the following attributes:

- Courage
- Intelligence
- Vision
- Commitment
- Attitude
- Persistence

Visit **www.thethreeadventurers.com** to learn more about "The Three Adventurers."

At fifty-eight, John Peck rowed across the Atlantic Ocean with very little rowing or nautical experience. He left La Gomera, a small Canary Island, and arrived nearly seventy days later in Barbados having rowed almost continuously two hours on and two hours off. John felt that commitment was important, so before leaving, he tore up his return air ticket meaning there was no way he was going to turn around and give up. He proved you can go a long way with a lot of small, insignificant steps — or strokes of the oars in his case. You can set an ambitious goal and achieve it. Although he didn't know much about rowing or being at sea, he managed the risk and the uncertainty. The rowing trip took nearly seventy days, whereas the preparation took the best part of eighteen months. He thought, he looked, he saw, he understood, he took action, and he achieved his goal. Through analysis he was able to assess what he did right and what he did wrong. What is interesting is that John's satisfaction comes not particularly from the rowing itself, which he describes as close to torture, but from the learning experience. John runs his successful consultancy business specializing in helping people unlock their potential.

Paul Bennett is a serial adventurer who also helps business people unlock their potential. Paul was a skipper in arguably the world's toughest yacht race, the BT Global Challenge, where identical steel yachts race around the world against the prevailing currents and winds. Paul's adventures have taught him that emotional intelligence is a defining factor in the achievement of team performance.

Adventure offers excitement and the prospect of achieving your dreams. You have to accept that while you can try to manage and control risk and uncertainty, the outcomes are not guaranteed, no matter how well you may prepare. Most people may think twice when they consider the worst that could happen and don't bother. If you learn to become a true adventurer, you will realize occasional failure is an occupational hazard. There is always something positive that can come out of the experience, even if it is simply deciding not to do the same thing again!

While researching the book and talking to many people about their business issues, the concepts of "business as an adventure" and "leadership in adventure" kept popping up. The spirit of adventure is behind mankind's greatest achievements: putting a man on the moon, the industrial and then technological revolutions, scientific discoveries etc. It has also been the power, inspiration, and motivation of some of the greatest businesses success stories. The spirit of adventure is still very much alive in many businesses, but in others it is critically ill, only just alive, or even dead!

Being a passionate adventurer myself, I feel that the spirit of adventure needs to be rediscovered, understood, and mastered to deliver exceptional performance. Adventure is one of the few topics that appear to have bypassed the corporate agenda. Society has become so risk-averse and frightened of change that it is holding back progress and great achievements. I believe we need big, exciting dreams and goals, and the courage to face risk and uncertainty and embark on worthwhile adventures. The spirit of adventure generates positive energy and excitement, which makes us feel good while also providing meaning and purpose. I believe that adventure is so important to business that I have established a new company, Leaders in Adventure Ltd, to focus entirely on this subject and, in particular, leadership of adventure.

The company provides six core services:

1. **Speakers and Seminars on Adventure:** to raise awareness and generate interest
2. **Research and Academic Development on Adventure:** to understand the issues
3. **Culture Change/Corporate Strategy Consultancy on Adventure:** to develop strategies to change the way people think
4. **Executive Coaching on Adventure:** to develop leadership in adventure
5. **Adventure Events:** to excite and reenergize employees
6. **Real Life Adventures:** to enable key individuals to grow and develop

Leaders in Adventure is a niche organization that aims to help key individuals encourage the spirit of adventure within their company, team, or group, change the way people think, and help them stretch to achieve business goals they thought were impossible. In particular, Leaders in Adventure helps people, especially leaders, manage risky and uncertain change situations:

- Maximizing business potential
- Helping organizations develop a winning culture
- Developing leadership through adventure

Leaders in Adventure works, typically, with a number of people handpicked by senior management for their positive attitude and enthusiasm, to develop and show them the way to get the spirit of adventure running through their organization's veins. Through adventure, people develop confidence and gain tools and coping strategies to win.

Until now, developing a positive attitude that enables people to take and manage risks and deal with uncertainty has been rare in the corporate environment. Contact Leaders in Adventure if you are interested in their services and share the values of:

- Boldness
- Trust
- Leadership
- Excitement

Further details can be found on www.leadersinadventure.com
enquiry@leadersinadventure.com

Leaders in Adventure
Embracing the Spirit of Adventure to Deliver Performance

Who are you and what do you want? If you know for sure, you are one of the lucky few, for the rest of us need to work it out for ourselves. Our life is a journey from birth to death. Our business is a journey from birth to death too. Fearful of death, we put it out of our minds and travel through life on the conveyor belt of time. Each day we live is one day closer to our death. Time is our most precious commodity, yet we waste so much following convention and others. Live for the present but plan for the future, for life is not a rehearsal. Have the courage to live your dreams, find your destiny, and leave your legacy.

CHAPTER 1
An Overview

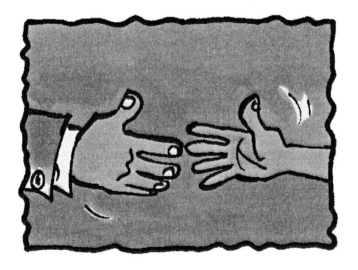

Opportunity and threat are the two key business drivers. Everyone loves opportunity, but who wants to deal with threats? Businesses exist to meet the needs of their owners/shareholders. Shareholders look to gain shareholder value, which is principally derived from profit or increased equity value. As a business leader you might own some or all of your business.

Business is becoming more competitive as the world, metaphorically speaking, is becoming a smaller place. The only real constant is continual change, threats around every corner, and the uncertainty of things we could once take for granted. The saying "survival of the fittest" can hardly be more relevant to today's business environment.

However, for every threat there is a new opportunity. We can approach the future with an element of fear and trepidation or we can boldly look forward to exciting and profitable times.

I believe business is like being on a journey that never ends; the challenge is the journey not the destination. If you think you have arrived you probably have nowhere to go. If you are not continually moving forward, you are probably going backwards. In other words doing nothing to advance and improve is not a viable option. Frequently business issues are not black and white and doing the right thing is often hard.

If achieving success in business were easy, everyone would do it. Today's directors and managers face a bewildering range of issues, where few things are straightforward. Technology is becoming an increasingly important factor in business success, yet while it creates the greatest opportunities, it also presents the greatest threats. The speed of change is so great that technology can be out of date before it's completely implemented. Technology itself can be highly confusing. Understanding the real issues against a backdrop of technology-vendor propaganda and misinformation can become an almost impossible task. The increasing cost of technology is also a significant issue.

 It is not just the technology that makes the difference, it is how it is used; it is also about people, attitudes, organization, process, timing, and much more.

THE BUSINESS CHALLENGE GAME

Business can be likened to a game that you play where winning is defined as both staying in the game (remaining in business) and succeeding (meeting the expectations of the owners). The world is full of hundreds of thousands of businesses that are at various stages (from formation to death). Most new businesses do not survive for more than a couple of years and the attrition rate continues over time. The rules of the game change continually although the guiding principles remain the same. The key principle is that to stay in business without continual investment you need to make profit, and the only way you can make profit is by ensuring that your sales revenues are greater than your costs.

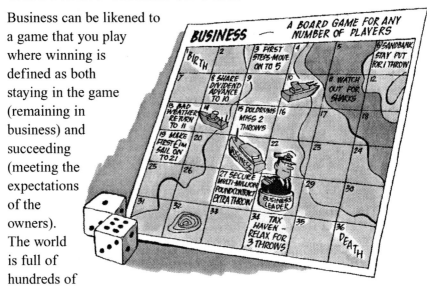

CONTROL

In any business you have to appreciate that some things are within your control and others are not. If one were to liken a business to a ship it would be up to its owners where to send it, what crew to have on board, what cargo to carry, etc. You can set your ship on its course towards its next destination with full knowledge of what speed she can sail and therefore, with an expectation of when she might arrive at the destination. If your engine breaks down or your ship runs into a storm or, worse still, hits the rocks, you are never going to make it to your destination. In the business context the storm might be the world economy, the engine breakdown failure might be failure of your manufacturing machines, and hitting the rocks might be running out of money. All businesses need to be designed to take the punishment from the conditions they might face.

HOW TO BECOME A GOOD PLAYER

If you are thinking of setting up a business, you need to realize that you and the crew you take with you on your journey need to be good at playing the business game. You have to understand the rules; you need a game plan that you need to be prepared to amend depending on the circumstances you face. You need courage, determination, intelligence, commitment, and plenty of energy.

 You must remember that in any business you have opponents. Your opponents will either be competitors or customers choosing to buy from neither you nor your competitors.

Ensure there is either a known need for the product and services you plan to supply or you are confident you can create that need.

Define your own strategy and your own rules. These are in addition to those imposed upon you such as government restrictions and laws, etc. You can be the David that beats Goliath or the tortoise that beats the hare.

THE LEAD OR FOLLOW CHOICE

 You can be the leader or you can take your chances and be the follower. If you pioneer a radical new concept you might learn the hard way and pay the price while your competitors learn from your mistakes and steal the advantage. Equally, if you follow you can miss the opportunity that others have taken first.

MOTIVATION TO PLAY

More than anything you have got to want to play the game and to accept with dignity the risks and reward that come with the territory.

If you lose the game you can always re-start or start a new game. The business game is played twenty-four hours a day, seven days a week, three hundred sixty-five days a year. In every country in the world, it never stops.

The game can be enjoyable, painful, enlightening, enriching, corrupting, and destroying, etc.

You set your own goals, you create your own vision for success, and you apply your own values.

THE BUSINESS GAMBLE

Business can be likened to gambling, where you have some influence over the outcomes, but not total control. You can place your money and efforts into a particular business venture, aimed at producing profits. You will either:

- Lose completely (lose all your money and waste all your efforts).
- Lose partially (lose some of your money but get something for your efforts).
- Break even (cover your costs, not making or losing anything).
- Win little (cover your costs and make a little).
- Win a lot (cover your costs and make a lot).

Most people want to win a lot, of course. Business, as in gambling, is all about a calculated or judged risk against an estimated or known return or benefit.

DIFFERENTIATION

For your business to succeed there has to be a demand for the products and services you are looking to sell. If one doesn't already exist, you need to create the demand.

Most businesses will have competitors — other businesses looking to sell the same or similar products or services to your potential customers. In some cases your biggest competitor is not another business, but potential customers who simply don't buy, i.e., the "do nothing" opponents.

Customer choice

Why should customers buy your products and services rather than someone else's? Why should they buy them rather than buy nothing? These are the questions you need to answer. Decide what factors customers will use in choosing, which might include:

- Price
- Quality
- Convenience
- Service and support
- Reputation
- Brand image, etc

Why difference is so important

The difference between you and your competition is everything. Frequently the differences are very small, but they make the difference between winning and loosing.

An analogy can be made with Formula One car racing. The rules are very strict; the engines have to be the same size, the weights have to be within closely defined tolerances, etc. The different teams spend tens of millions of dollars designing and building cars. In races the first three cars might finish a seventy-minute race within five seconds of each other. For all the effort that goes into the cars, and the driver selection, what is it that accounts for those five seconds? Is it the fitness of the drivers, a screw that is not flush and is spoiling the aerodynamics, or something else? The race is not about the seventy minutes, it's all about the five seconds, the difference between winning and loosing. In motor racing there are prizes for second and third places, but not in business; you either win the order or lose it, it is as simple as that.

Small things do matter

When looking for differentiation, it is easy for novices to focus on the big exciting things, the new computer system perhaps, or the corporate brochure. The reality is that the differences are often very small. On their own they may seem almost insignificant, but when added together they make the difference.

Make your business, not your product or service, the deciding factor

Customers tend to be naturally product or service centered. Their need is for your products and services, not your company. Fighting the competitive game on products or services alone is the most difficult and the most likely to lead to "lowest price" scenarios.

Do everything in your power to raise the stakes, put value in front of price and sell your company first and your products and services later. Your products and services might be easy for your competitors to imitate, your company isn't. Let your customers know why dealing with your company will be one of the best decisions they ever made and that they will never regret it.

WORDS OF WISDOM

The small things do matter, attention to detail is important as is the quest for continual improvement.

However good you are, you can always be better.

OPPORTUNITY VERSUS THREAT

Imagine wealth beyond your wildest dreams, executive jets, extravagant super yachts, and houses like palaces, exotic cars, and luxury surrounding every part of your life. All this is possible as a result of the success of your business. But is this what you want? Would you rather have health, security, close family, and friends?

You can have whatever you want. It is for you to decide, but remember everything has its price. What pleasure can wealth offer without someone to share it? What would life be like with nothing to look forward to? Surely, making other people happy brings happiness to you. The world is full of opportunity if you are prepared to look for it.

Imagine, now, losing all your possessions and all your money, your home, your lifestyle, your friends and family, or your health.

How much are you prepared to risk in your quest to grasp opportunities and establish your own business. Only you can decide. Balance opportunity and reward against threats and risks.

TRUST

Trust is the delivery of expectation. Would you deal with a business you didn't trust? You may or may not; it would probably depend upon the circumstances, the alternatives available to you, the perceived risk and your level of urgency. If your car has broken down in a remote village and you are at the only garage for hundreds of

miles, you might consider using them even if you know their work is known to be sub-standard quality, and they are known to overcharge.

For your business to take advantage of opportunities, potential customers have to believe that the business will make good its promises. Most customers are trusting. It is human nature to give others the benefit of the doubt, but it is easy for customers to become ex-customers. If trust has been breached, the situation needs to be remedied to the customer's satisfaction. Real trust has to be earned by delivering against expectations, but it is possible to gain trust in other ways including:

- Recommendation/referrals
- Testimonials from others
- Third party accreditation (e.g., ISO 9000)
- Membership of trade organizations
- Partnerships with well-known companies
- Good publicity
- Qualifications
- Track record of the business participants (e.g., directors, employees, shareholders)

WORDS OF WISDOM

Customers naturally want to trust you; make it easy for them by showing them proof continually.

Continual change is the only certainty

 As human beings we are naturally creatures of habit. We like routine and structure — just look at any society throughout the world. The business world, however, is one where change is an important element. Effectively embracing and managing the process of change is one of the greatest business issues of our generation. The business world runs contrary to many of our natural instincts.

Laws of supply and demand

The laws of supply and demand underpin the business world. It is all about buying and selling and adding value in the process. The desire to buy is demand; the ability to sell and deliver is supply. Competitive advantage is the factor that enables a business to be successful selling its products or services against its competitors. The best competitive advantage is monopoly where there are no competitors. If you have a unique product or service for which there is a demand, you might be able to achieve monopoly. However, once others — your competitors — see the opportunity they may well copy or even improve upon your products and services. For this reason competitive advantage is normally short lived, hence the need for continual change. Most countries have laws that ban monopolies.

PROFIT DRIVER

Given a key element of business success is profit, which is achieved by having sales revenues greater than costs, supply and demand impacts the sales side of the equation. Costs are derived from purchase prices and operational efficiency, which form the other key element of profit.

Revenue/Cost factors

In simple terms, to increase the success of your business you can either increase your sales revenue, reduce your costs, or a combination of both. The route to achieve this has taxed the minds of the world's leading scholars and most exceptional businessmen since the creation of commerce. There is more understanding and knowledge available today than there ever has been in the history of mankind, which is the good news. The bad news is that the increased understanding and knowledge raise the stakes and increase the rate of change. This means that successful businessmen of the future need to embrace the concept with open arms and make sure they become and remain the winners, not the losers.

BUSINESS CONCEPTS

Business thrives on new concepts, new ideas, and new approaches to old problems. Good business leaders are continually searching for the next new thing that is going to improve their lives and their business fortunes. There are so many issues in the business world, however, that seeing the big picture can be difficult, if not impossible.

Go into any major bookstore and in the business books section you will see a huge array of books that address different business-related topics. I suggest there is very little that is genuinely new and never been thought of before.

Old concepts seem to be continually reinvented and new ones merge into each other. There is little doubt that there is huge demand for knowledge and that many business people in all industries and sizes of business are looking for guidance and answers. When these are available in plentiful supply, the issue becomes why in most instances are the changes in results so small?

The benefits of new business concepts cancel one another, when many businesses implement them. The secret is to implement them quicker to gain temporary advantage and implement them better to gain greater benefits.

IMPORTANT BUSINESS RULES

Rule number 1

Sales revenues need to be greater than costs to achieve profit. If sales revenues are less than costs, the result will be losses. Profit is the most important business success indicator.

Rule number 2

Choice is the defining business factor. As a business leader the choices you make define the outcomes you receive. Make the right choices and you will be successful, make the wrong choices or fail to make choices at all and you will not.

Rule number 3

Nothing can be achieved without action. Having made a choice, you need to be able to fully implement it.

Rule number 4

Having taken action, you need to measure and assess the results and make new choices and take new actions.

Rule number 5

There are only three things that you can influence to increase sales:

- Win more customers.
- Sell them more products and services.
- Do it more often.

CONTINUED →

....

WORDS OF WISDOM

Business is about adding value.

The only things that are right are those that work.

What worked in the past or present is not guaranteed to work in the future.

The only way you will know what will work is by doing it.

The only certainty is continual change.

Business is all about choice: Do something or do nothing.

New concepts are often old ones relabeled.

....

THE BUSINESS CIRCLE

Business achievements are normally the result of decisions and actions. Every day of your business life you need to make choices and decisions and take actions. It is all about:

- Knowing what to do (choices/decisions)
- Doing what you need to do (actions)
- Measuring/assessing results and making new decisions (analysis and review)

Knowing the right things to do can be hard, but it can be even harder to complete the actions, particularly when other people are involved.

As a business leader, it is your job to understand what to do, to do what needs to be done, and to measure and assess the results. You need to take responsibility and stand accountable. This comes with the territory; it is the price you have to pay.

THE BUSINESS CYCLE

Like products and services, businesses have life cycles. They are born when they are created and they eventually die when they are shut down or go bust. The alternative is that they are merged with other businesses, where they may lose their old identity and characteristics and gain new ones. They may also be broken into parts and sold off in bits to either merge with other businesses or to form the catalyst for new businesses.

BUSINESS STAGES

Depending upon the business they may go through various stages:

- Birth
- Maturity
- Growth
- Decline
- Stagnation
- Death

BUSINESSES AS ORGANIZATIONS

Businesses are just one form of organization, which exist to fulfill a purpose, namely delivering shareholder value, which usually means profit. Business success relies on the organization functioning well.

Some governments consider businesses good organizations. They extol the virtues of businesses, suggesting that they could do a better job of running some public services than government organizations.

There are many different types of organizations, such as schools, hospitals, government, charities, clubs and societies, but one type of organization stands out as being particularly highly effective, and that is military organizations.

THINKING OUTSIDE THE BOX: LEARNING FROM UNEXPECTED SOURCES

Why are the military so good at organizing and achieving their objectives? What secrets do they use that we can use in business? When the chips are down, the military come into their own, they have made an art and science out of organizational effectiveness. Good military organizations work, they achieve the impossible and often make it look easy.

As a Royal Naval Officer, I have had the pleasure of serving her Majesty in what I consider to be one of the finest military organizations in the world. I learned a huge amount about myself; I developed in many different ways, experienced exceptional responsibility at an early age and would recommend the experience to anyone.

THE BOYHOOD OF MANY A SUCCESSFUL BUSINESSMAN

At the time I considered a short career commission in the Royal Navy would provide a better grounding to a career in business than a business studies degree. I felt that if it was good enough for members of the British Royal Family then it was certainly good enough for me. I joined one or two years after Prince Andrew. I believed that the leadership and management skills I would acquire from the Royal Navy would give me competitive advantage in the business world. In reality, my short Royal Naval career gave me a whole lot more.

> *"I have determined to try ... for well we know that if a person does not perform as he promises, the world is very apt to say he never did intend to do it."* — Admiral Nelson 1785

WHY DO GOOD MILITARY ORGANIZATIONS WORK SO WELL?

From my own experience in the Royal Navy, I have deduced that the following ingredients combine together to make the Royal Navy such an effective organization:

Selection

Out of all the selection processes I have been through in my life, none has been as thorough as I experienced when joining the Royal Navy. The process starts with an expression of interest, the provision of comprehensive written information, and an interview with a Royal Navy Careers Officer. This interview creates a sell-sell opportunity for both the Royal Navy Careers Officer to sell the benefits of a Royal Navy career and set expectations and also for the applicants to sell themselves as potentially suitable material. Honesty and openness is encouraged. Much of the questioning of the candidate is geared to life experience, life purpose, and long-term goals. Should the candidate wish to proceed further, he or she is asked to complete a very detailed application form that requires considerable forethought. The emphasis is about embarking upon a selection process as well as a preparation process.

Becoming an officer in Her Majesty's Royal Navy is not an easy thing to do. The barriers to entry are deliberately high to prevent insincere applicants from conning their way in. Royal Navy recruiters know exactly what they are looking for, which is not, as some may imagine, a typecast clone profile. The case is quite the contrary. They recognize the need for variety. They are, however, looking for the potential in people. This could be leadership, courage, fortitude, determination, intelligence, honor, integrity, and aptitude for the functional roles one might fulfill and, last of all, enthusiasm.

Application forms can be submitted only with the approval of a Royal Navy Careers Officer. Applications are reviewed centrally and applicants are invited to an intensive two-day selection program. Applicants spend an entire day doing a wide variety of written tests, including psychological and psychometric, as well as math, English, and other tests. The second day includes practical leadership tests with ropes, barrels, planks, etc., over pools of ice-cold water and a series of interviews with a variety of different people, including a psychologist.

The final interview is with the Admiralty Interview Board, comprising a panel of senior naval officers and a schools headmaster. Never in my life have I been through a more demanding interview. The combined level of knowledge and the sharpness of the questioning would expose almost any shortcomings or lies. If you say you want the join the Royal Navy to see the world, they will point to a blank map of the world and ask you to identify say, Afghanistan, Yemen, or St. Helena. The detailed application form has been checked and verified, there is no opportunity for artistic license. They adopt a point-based marking system that enables them to objectively select who they consider to be the best candidates.

WORDS OF WISDOM
Be slow to hire, quick to fire.

Training
The Royal Navy invests in people. It is committed to the professional and personal development of all its personnel. When recruiting, they look for some of the following attributes:

- Attitude
- Knowledge
- Motivation
- Intelligence
- Competency
- Personality

Standards
Standards are everything, only the best will do. This impacts every area imaginable from professional practices to standards of dress code to the tidiness of your dirty laundry basket.

Rules

The Queen's regulations for the Royal Navy are about six inches thick and define rules for everything imaginable.

CONTINUED →

Teamwork

Teamwork is absolutely essential. There is no room for loners or individualists.

Assessments

Everything is assessed, measured and recorded. Continual improvement is required and there is a major focus on achievement. Winning is everything.

Development and progression

The system for development and progression is clearly and fairly laid out and practiced properly.

Caring and welfare

While the demands for commitment are high, the Royal Navy looks after its own, and considerable effort is

placed on the welfare of the individual. Their families are supported and even their religious and spiritual well-being has a high priority.

Practice and rehearsal

Military drill is well recognized. Everything is practiced and rehearsed time and time again until it is second nature.

Organizational hierarchy and command and control

There is no confusion over organizational hierarchy and command and control. You know very clearly who to take orders from

and who to give orders to.

Process

Processes work like clockwork. In every ship in the Fleet, the same processes are adhered to. Ships change their crews regularly and they continue to function with a seamless transition.

Communication

Every aspect of communication is well thought out. The layout of letters and memos is defined in a writing guide, orders are given in particular ways, and information is disseminated on control notice boards that the crew is obliged to read. Ship-to-ship and ship-to-shore communications are superbly controlled, as are tactical battlefield communications. Even information broadcasts on the ship's Tannoy system are done in a particular way.

Delegation and accountability

Dovetailing into the organizational hierarchy and command and control systems are methods of delegation and systems of accountability.

Competition

Competition is encouraged at every level in almost every activity or situation. It's all about being the best, the winner.

Recognition and reward

Recognition and reward systems are structured and fair. Ask anyone who has been awarded a medal whether they are proud to hold it, and the answer will be undoubtedly "yes" because it means something worthwhile.

Common purpose
Defending one's Queen and country is a noble cause. Liberating the oppressed, defending the vulnerable and upholding values and traditions bond the organization to a higher purpose.

Division of labor

Who does what, when, and how is clearly defined. Even though you may be a marine engineer or mechanic, you are still required to help store the ship of ammunition, sacks of potatoes, etc.

Discipline
Discipline binds the organization together, by enforcing the rules. Compliance is not optional; rules have purpose, even if you don't necessarily understand them.

Honesty and truth
Honesty and truth are values, which are never compromised.

"Nothing which ought to be attempted should be left undone."
— Admiral Nelson, 1799

THE POWER OF SYSTEMS

As I think back to my time in the Royal Navy, I am able to see so much now that I couldn't see then. When you are in the system, you take it for granted, you play your part and you live the Royal Navy life. It is of course not all rosy, there are grumbles and complaints but it works and it works well. When you are at wars, winning or losing means the difference between life and death, kill or be killed. I can promise you, this focuses attention.

HEADS I WIN, TAILS YOU LOSE

When people join, of course, they don't see the end result as their dying. Dying can spoil your day. The risks are real, as I know only too well.

When I left Britannia Royal Naval College, I was appointed to the HMS Coventry. I received my joining instructions and formally accepted my appointment. A few days before I was due to join her, she sailed for the South Atlantic to join the Falklands War. She was the second ship to be sunk with a loss of forty lives. If I had been due to join just a few days earlier, I would have been on her. In the military, the risks are real and the stakes are high.

You might think the above analysis has very little relevance to you establishing or running your own business. I believe that many of the secrets to business success are revealed in the phenomenal military system. Despite what many might think, the similarities between military and business organizations and systems are remarkably similar.

Military advantage can be related to competitive advantage, with one exception. It's more important to win in the military than it is in business. In business you can lose your money but in the military you can lose your life. Remarkably the greatest rewards in life are fulfillment, satisfaction and happiness, not money. The military doesn't pay as well as business, the commitments and workloads are usually significantly higher, but being part of a professional team that you are proud to represent is priceless. Much of the business world is about mediocrity, while the military world is about excellence. Those who have served will know what I mean; those who haven't should try it, but everyone should be able to learn lessons from the military systems that they can apply to their own businesses.

THE CONCLUSION

The things that make good military organizations so successful are very similar to the things that make good businesses successful. Military and business objectives might be different, but both are focused on achievement and success. Behind each organization is a system of operation. It is this system, which holds the answers and links together the many different factors.

REAL-LIFE STORY

I was selected to join the Royal Navy as one of an intake of a hundred sixty from approximately 20,000 applications. Of those selected, six of us were on an experimental three-and-a-half-year, short career commission and of those, I was the youngest and the only non-graduate. Our training time was cut in half, but the examinations remained the same. At age twenty I joined a ship as the youngest compliment officer in the fleet. Within a very short time I was Officer of the Watch of a £50 million warship with approximately three hundred crewmembers; this meant being on the bridge in charge of the ship and all who sailed with her.

One night while I was officer of the watch, we were shadowing a very impressive Russian warship, which was steaming between the Shetland and Faeroes Islands. My orders were to maintain station one mile astern of the Russian ship. Every now and again I would check the radar screen to measure the distance and adjust speed as necessary. As I sat comfortably in the captain's chair, the stern lights of the Russian warship looked brighter. She had, in fact, stopped dead in the water and I was steaming at fifteen knots straight for her.

Quick action avoided disaster. Imagine the international repercussions of a Royal Naval warship ramming or even sinking a Russian destroyer. Only I avoided the disaster, there was no one looking over my shoulder saying, "Look out!" Why was it the crew had total confidence that their young, inexperienced officer was not going to kill them? They rightly believed in the system and the system worked. Things obviously can go wrong and they invariably will from time to time. After I left my last Royal Naval ship, the HMS Guernsey, it ran onto the rocks when approaching Aberdeen in the United Kingdom and nearly sunk. Over twelve feet of water filled the engine room. When things go wrong, it's absolutely critical to have a system in place to deal with it.

To explore is to look and seek, for it is only by doing this that you will actually see and discover. Discovery is one of mankind's greatest purposes, which generates satisfaction beyond one's wildest dreams. Everyone should be an explorer.

CHAPTER 2:
Self-Understanding

THE SECRETS OF SELF-UNDERSTANDING

I love the challenge and excitement of business and am fascinated by it. I feel compelled to learn more and explore new areas. I feel like the equivalent of a religious scholar in search of the Holy Grail, seeking out the secrets of business success. In all the business situations I have experienced and witnessed, I look for the factors that lead to success. As I look through business book stores at the massive volume of knowledge and information that is on offer, and consider the collective intelligence of the world's most learned and knowledgeable academics who devote their lives to the subject, I am left wondering why it is that business success is so hard to achieve with such incredible resources available. Both big and small businesses have difficulty achieving the success they desire on a long-term basis.

Business success will always depend on a large number of different factors, which have differing amounts of importance in differing circumstances. People look to the past to see what has worked before, but they often don't appreciate that the circumstances have to be the same for them to work in the future. One of the few certainties in business is continual change. It is unlikely circumstances from the past will be the same in the future. Is it surprising, therefore, that business success is hard to maintain?

WORDS OF WISDOM

We search wide and far for answers, but they mostly lie within us if we look hard enough.

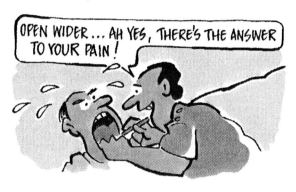

Many secrets of business success exist in the business leader's self-understanding. Answers to business problems are locked within these

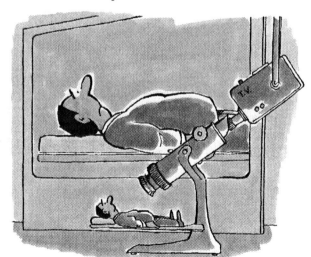

people, many who are struggling to find them. How frustrating it is to have the answers, but not be able to see them? The answer is "very," which is why some people are reading this book now.

HOW HUMAN BEINGS INTERFERE WITH THEIR OWN ABILITY TO ACHIEVE AND LEARN

Mental obstacles can prevent maximum performance. I am sure we have all experienced a mental block, our minds letting us down just at the time that we need them most. It might be the fumbled presentation, the missed sale, the lost opportunity. Everything might have been so right for us to achieve, but something about our inner self let us down.

Every game has two parts, the inner game and the outer game. The outward game is played against opponents to reach a goal or outcome. The inner game is that that which takes place in our minds and might involve:

Negative:

- Self-doubt
- Lack of concentration and focus
- Nervousness
- Self-condemnation: "I'm going to lose, I know I am."

Positive:

- Self-confidence
- Self-belief
- Spontaneous performance and achievement
- Calmness
- Focus

The inner and outer game

Nowhere is the inner and outer game more obvious than sport. The difference between winning sportsmen and their opponents is often remarkably small. There is something about the best sportsmen that is difficult to properly define. They just seem to exude self-confidence; they convince themselves and others of the outcome before they even start. Examples are Mohammed Ali in boxing, Michael Schumacher in motor racing, Tiger Woods in golf, Bjorn Borg and the Williams sisters in tennis, and five-time Olympic gold medalist, Steve Redgrave in rowing. When these sportsmen were in their prime, nobody doubted their ability to win. They expected it. So strong was the psyche that one sometimes wonders why their opponents even bothered turning up. They all have their day until a new upstart comes along and knocks them off their perch.

Being mentally prepared to win

The one thing that stands out about these people is that their minds seem calm and at one with their bodies. Inside they have a will to win, which unlocks an inner energy, which is never diminished by losing. It is interesting to see that this inner energy is not everlasting, it eventually runs out and the results are obvious for everyone to see. It's as if these people have an inner pot of winning serum. Occasionally it seems to empty and their predictable winning turns to losing. For some, it momentarily returns and for others, it is gone forever.

Scientific explanation

There is a logical and scientific explanation for this phenomenon. As psychologists know we all have a conscious and subconscious mind. Our subconscious mind helps us to learn to walk and talk when we are children, while our conscious mind lives in the reality of today and makes the conscious choices of which we are all aware. Anyone who understands biology will know there are different parts of our brain, which control different parts of our body and thinking.

What happens is that our subconscious minds have everything we need to win and succeed, but our conscious minds dominate and therefore prevent us reaching full potential.

How to let your subconscious mind take control

To allow our natural subconscious mind to allow us to win, we need to stop our conscious minds from interfering with it.

How often in life do you find you rehearse something and it all goes well, then you do the same thing when it matters and it all seems to go wrong? Think of a golfer on the driving range who places ball after ball just where he wants it, and then goes out to play a match and the ball goes everywhere. Another example is when football strikers take penalties. Many people would agree that the mental side of sports is important, but exactly the same is true in business and your private life. It doesn't have to be a physical activity. Just think of the top chess players who play a psychological game as big as their chess game. Think, too, about the military. It's of paramount importance to play the game convinced you are going to win.

Have you ever been driving your car and suddenly realize you can't remember what you have been doing for the last ten or fifteen minutes and yet somehow you are still on the road? You have been responding subconsciously to dangers. How do you think motor-racing drivers can cope when events happen in split seconds? It's all down to the subconscious mind, the inner self.

Understanding your two selves

By now you will have realized that you have in essence two different minds, your conscious mind and your subconscious mind. Our ability to manage the relationship between our two minds is the key factor in determining our ability to translate knowledge of technique into effective action.

Our subconscious mind, which includes our nervous system, hears everything, sees everything, senses everything, and is highly intelligent. Our conscious mind on the other hand tends to be responsible for most of our actions.

Our subconscious minds are the truly knowledgeable ones and should tell our conscious minds what to do. Our conscious minds should listen to what our subconscious minds tell us and do it. The problem lies in the fact that our conscious minds don't completely trust our subconscious minds and question what they are being told. When our conscious minds do too much telling, things start to go wrong, which generates feelings of uncertainty and doubt, lack of self-confidence and self-esteem. It's at this point that our self-belief starts to walk out the door. Once into this cycle, it's very difficult to break. Our conscious minds are trying too hard and are over-ruling our subconscious minds. It is possible to try too hard.

The secret is to try and focus your conscious mind not on the task, but on achieving the outcome. It's all about visualizing the action as it should be that results in the desired outcome. As soon as you program your mind with images rather than with words and start to trust your subconscious mind, you will find that things will start to come together.

LET YOUR SUBCONSCIOUS MIND TAKE CONTROL

D.T. Suzuki, the renowned Zen master, describes the effect of the conscious mind on archery in his foreword to Zen and the Art of Archery:

"As soon as we reflect, deliberate, and conceptualize, the original unconsciousness is lost and the thought interferes.... The arrow is off the string but does not fly straight to the target, nor does the target stand where it is. Calculation, which is miscalculation, sets in.

Man is a thinking reed, but his great works are done when he is not calculating and thinking. Childlikeness has to be restored with long years of training in self-forgetfulness."

This whole subject is psychology, but there is an uncanny truth behind these phenomena. Psychologists talk about going back to the childlike state where the unconscious is predominant. Perhaps this is one area in life where we don't progress as much as we think we do.

Dr. Maria Montessori, a well-known educator, dedicated a lifetime to discovering how and why children learn. A scientist by background, she was Italy's first doctor to apply scientific research and techniques to children's mental and spiritual development. When we look at her discoveries from the perspective of self-understanding of adults, we begin to understand why certain things happen. The unpredictable and chaotic world is more predictable and more orderly than we might imagine.

The subconscious mind is natural. When it causes us to act, it is with spontaneity. Interestingly, Dr. Montessori saw great importance in nature and felt that, "Civilized man is a contented prisoner, in a sanitized world." Our souls and spirits have shrunk and filled out minds with contradiction as we have moved from the natural to the man made world. Is it any surprised that we find our modern world chaotic and unpredictable? There is so much to learn from Dr. Montessori that I

commend her works, for they will provide you with many explanations
for the unexplainable. She makes sense of the chaotic world.

> "*The importance of work does not bother children, they are
> satisfied when they have done as much as they can and see that
> they are not excluded from an opportunity to exert themselves in
> their surroundings. The most admired work is that which offers
> the greatest opportunities to each one. They have a kind of inner
> ambition which consists of bringing into full play the talents that
> God has given them, as in the gospel parable; and when they
> succeed in this, they arouse the admiration of many others.*"
> — Maria Montessori

How to achieve and learn

While we continually look to the future, we already hold many of the
secrets, locked in our past. To overcome the conflict between your
conscious and subconscious minds, you need to find ways of training
your conscious mind to trust your subconscious mind. This is easier said
than done because distrust causes you to try too hard.

Later in this chapter, under the Wisdom section, we will discuss
techniques for doing this by gaining a greater self-consciousness. It is as
important to be relaxed and self-confident as it is to be healthy. Intuition
is the subconscious mind talking to us; we should try to listen to it more
often. Fear is one of the greatest reasons; our conscious minds don't
trust our subconscious minds. You can overcome fear, by putting in
perspective the worst that can happen. For example, providing the worst
did happen, could you survive? Could you handle the consequences? If
the answer is yes, you should try not to worry about it. Fear creates
pressure, which in turn creates stress. This can be a good thing in small
doses, it helps us achieve, but in big doses it can be highly destructive.

 An effective way to cope with stress is to face it head on by breaking it
down into manageable chunks. Use these steps for coping with stress:

❏ Write down a list with three columns. In the first column, write a
list of all the things that cause you stress. In the second column
make a note whether there is anything you can do to stop the
thing that is causing you stress. In the third column write a list of
all the things that you could do to stop or reduce the stress.

❏ Rank the things you could do in order of what effect you think they might have, with number one having the most effect and so on.

❏ Do the things that would reduce the stress in priority order.

❏ Where you can't do anything to reduce the stress, ask your friends or work colleagues if they have any ideas.

❏ If there is nothing you can do to reduce that particular stress, accept that you can't and stop worrying about it. Try to remember, "What will be, will be," and "You can only do as much as you can do."

❏ Review your list regularly and take what action is appropriate.

 Remember: If something has gone wrong, it provides an excellent opportunity to learn from it. In every failure is the seed of equal or greater success.

LIFE PROGRESSION

Our lives are all about progression; time is the common factor that we all share. We progress through our life from the day we are born; we  grow mentally and physically through our childhood. Our bodies change over time in adulthood and there is probably a stage at which we reach our physical peak. Athletes are probably more aware of this than most. Steve Redgrave won gold medals in five consecutive Olympic rowing games, an astounding achievement. He did not intend to attempt a sixth because he knew he would be physically past his best and unable to compete with young people at an earlier stage in their lives.

MENTAL AND SPIRITUAL PROGRESSION

Mentally and spiritually we can continue to develop to a much older age. In terms of physical development our bodies wear out like a machine, they can get damaged or break down. Our bodies can be likened to a bank where we are continually making withdrawals until the account is empty. Conversely, with our minds we are predominantly making deposits of knowledge and experience. It is interesting to note that when our minds start to deteriorate, often in old age, it is usually a result of the physical deterioration of our brains. The brain is merely a part of our body's machine that hosts our mind.

Mental and spiritual maturity have a major impact on the performance of business leaders and, therefore, the success of business itself. Emotional intelligence has been recognized as a major factor of effective leadership and success. This is discussed later in the "Business Voyage" chapter.

WISDOM

As a business leader your mental and spiritual progression is far more important than your physical condition. The three important aspects are:

- Knowledge
- Skill
- Experience

These three combined enable the creation of wisdom, which is "knowledge of what is true or right coupled with judgment as to action," which is referred to by some as "common sense."

The above descriptions may sound a little academic and detached from the real world, but being successful in business is about having good understanding, making the right decisions, taking the right actions, and learning from the outcomes.

Unlocking your wisdom within

Wisdom comes from consciousness and from consciousness comes self-awareness and from self-awareness comes the power to understand and make changes.

An exercise to increase consciousness

Business leaders' lives are busy, typified by too much work and too little time. In the hustle and bustle of everyday life, it is difficult to stop and increase your consciousness. Use this five-minute exercise to raise your consciousness:

- Sit in a chair. Sit straight as if your spine is a pole standing tall and erect.

- Place your feet slightly apart, with the soles of your feet completely flat on the ground.

- Now drop your shoulders and close your eyes.

- Feel the weight of your body on the chair.

- Feel the weight of your clothes on your back.

- Hear the furthest sound but don't hold onto it.

- See colors in your mind and sense any smells.

- Be conscious and remain like that for four minutes.

Doing this exercise will help you relax your mind, become aware of all your senses, and raise your consciousness. Notice how it improves your ability to deal with your busy life.

THE ESCALATOR OF LIFE

Imagine your life as an escalator, where you get on at the bottom and the escalator starts to take you upwards. We would all love to think that our life progression is all forwards and upwards. For most people the truth is somewhat different in that there are times when we move onward and upward only to find that there are times when we go downward and backward before starting the upward progression again. We have all heard the expression "three steps forward, two steps back."

REACHING THE TOP

It is human nature that we need to advance and progress and reach the top; it is this desire that motivates us to do the things that we do. In most business environments, participants will be remunerated partially based on experience as well as actual performance. Experience counts for something but performance will always be the defining factor.

Human beings, by nature, are creatures of habit and we all, to different extents, conform to the ways of the world in which we live. Career paths and life paths are defined by convention and common practice. We all get on to our career escalators and life escalators and try to ride them upward. Once on them we are very reluctant to get off. I believe our lives could be enriched and improved by sometimes getting off these escalators of conformity and setting new personal and career paths.

It is all about taking a new perspective, stepping outside your comfort zone, and thinking long and hard about what you want to get out of your business and private life.

FEAR OF GETTING OFF

There is always a fear that if you get off your escalators, you will not be able to get back on or that any new escalators you find will not be as good. The drivers are fear, combined with security, and gain. Getting off your escalator, which might mean resigning a highly paid job with a structured career progression, is a potentially risky business. Renting out the family home and sailing around the world for three years might mean little or no income and three years wasted, while others seize the opportunities you have given up, but alternatively, the rewards of quality family time and the life enriching experiences and adventures could vastly outweigh anything you might have lost.

THE BENEFITS OF GETTING OFF AND STARTING AGAIN

Even if you do not want to radically change your life, you might find that getting off your escalator and starting at a lower level, even doing the same thing, could give you the opportunity to learn from your past experiences, which is likely to increase your chances of greater success. By definition, entrepreneurs get off their career escalators when they establish their own businesses.

The bottom line is that as far as we can confidently tell we only get one life, it is not a rehearsal. Therefore, you need to think very carefully about the paths you want to take. There are no rights and wrongs. It is your life to do with as you see fit.

As a business leader you need to consider that your employees are on their life and career escalators and they might need to get off to develop and progress themselves. Self-progression is a very powerful motivator. Can you give people career and personal development within your organization? Can you help your employees to define where they want to be and what they want to achieve? Can you align your employees' interests with your own? Are you giving enough consideration at recruitment time to where your employees need to go? Do you want somebody who has reached a level at which they are perfectly comfortable? Everyone reaches a stage where they do not want to advance and progress, they are happy with their lot. You need to understand this from your own perspective, but also the perspective of your employees.

If you take the trouble to look ahead, it is normally possible to anticipate what things you need to do to enable you to achieve the outcomes you desire. This might be professional examinations, experience in different roles, or the development of knowledge and skills. You have to remember that you are in control of your own life, even if you have to accept external factors beyond your control.

DON'T LET YOUR ESCALATOR OF LIFE TURN INTO A TREADMILL YOU CAN'T GET OFF

Have you ever felt like you are working like mad and achieving little or nothing? Do you ever feel that you are like a hamster on a treadmill going nowhere? I think most people feel like this at some stage in their life. For some the rise in fame and fortune seems steady and unstoppable, but for the ordinary person, the upward rise is rarely smooth and consistent.

If you find yourself in a "getting nowhere" phase, take stock and consider what you might do differently, how you might change course and seek alternative paths.

....

WORDS OF WISDOM

Never accept that you can't do anything about your current situation, there is always an alternative if you look hard enough and are brave enough.

....

CAREER AND LIFE FLIGHT PATH MANAGEMENT

Our life path is the time between our birth and death. Our career path is the time from commencing work to retirement. If we accept the concept that our career and life paths are progressions, we can make the analogy with an airplane taking off.

The airplane needs to be mechanically sound and have enough fuel and a pilot who is in control. The airplane taxis along to the end of the runway. The pilot then pushes the throttles to full power. The airplane builds up speed until there is enough air speed to enable the plane to take off. The plane then climbs to its cruising altitude, travels as far as the fuel will allow it and the pilot chooses to take it, then descends and lands on another runway. Once the wheels have touched the ground, the pilot slams on the brakes and puts the engine into reverse thrust until the plane has come to a complete standstill. Along the route, the plane might have encountered some bad weather such as turbulence or strong headwinds, or air traffic control might have altered its route, all of which are out of the pilot's control.

 If you understand these concepts, you should realize you have influence over your own flight path. By taking a step back from your own day-to-day world and looking forward to your future career and life path, you can empower yourself, gain greater fulfillment, and enjoy greater success.

REAL-LIFE STORY

My sister-in-law, Catherine Denning (nee Gratwicke), was stuck in a rut, unhappy and unappreciated at work. She created woven textile designs, a job that requires considerable skills but that paid appallingly.

Like so many people, she pondered her future and asked herself the questions "who am I and what do I want?" For her, the answer was not clear. She knew she needed a career direction change, but she was not quite sure exactly what. Initially, she thought about graphic design, but ruled it out because it would mean retraining. She then had a feeling she might like to do photography, a medium she had been using for years as a means of inspiration for her woven fabrics. It seemed obvious — photography was the way forward.

Using a camera she had had for years, she started taking pictures. I had always noticed that Cath would snap away at the most unlikely subjects. I remember clearly when we were working on my yacht one weekend in a boatyard in Southampton, she started taking snapshots of some rusty cans lying on the stony ground. It's interesting to remember that I introduced Cath to another friend of mine, Ellen MacArthur, an aspiring young British sailor whose story I tell later in the book.

The idea of earning a living with photography grew in her mind. I never understood what she wanted to do. I believe when many of us think of photographers, we think of weddings or maybe family portraits, or perhaps journalistic or marketing photography, glamour, and so on. There are so many different types of photography.

I remember her considering going to college or getting a job as a photographer's assistant so she could learn the trade. Eventually, she did work as a photographer's assistant for a few months, but again she was frustrated by the way she was treated. She had to spend more time making the tea and lunch, cleaning, carrying the bags, and simply taking the blame when the shoot went wrong than taking pictures.

Many people would have given up and found something easier to do, but not Cath, for the more she looked at the market, the more she thought she wanted to be a part of it, despite her experiences.

So what should she do? Go to college to study photography and join others on the starting rungs as an assistant to another photographer? Should she give up and do something else or forge ahead with what she wanted, regardless of what anyone else thought?

Using the photos she took at work for various textile companies and a few personal photos, Cath put together a respectable portfolio. Initially, she took these around to show to lots of interior and fashion magazines. The response was overwhelming, and she started to get a few commissions. Her life became a roller coaster quickly gathering momentum. She set up a business and decided she would take her destiny into her own hands and try to sell her services directly.

Cath took charge of her life. She searched inside for answers that took time to surface. She stepped off her life's escalator, leaving one career without actually having firm plans of exactly what to do next. She refused to stay on a treadmill that for her was going nowhere. Now Cath is a highly respected interior, still life, and lifestyle photographer. Her work is in great demand, and she commands very high fees, a world away from her low salary as a fabric designer. She does work for international magazines such as *Homes and Gardens*, *Country Living*, and *Marie Claire*. Unlike others, she didn't start a new career at the bottom of a new escalator, but decided to get on nearer the top.

Call it a lucky break, perhaps, but early in her new photography career as a complete unknown with little prior experience, she was commissioned by Marie Claire magazine to do a project. She found herself working with a very well-known stylist named Leslie. What she didn't realize was that this was Leslie Dilcock, whose work had partly inspired Cath to become an interior photographer. She became very nervous when she found out, but it all worked out well and the rest is history.

I happen to think we all make our luck, and I think this is true of Cath. Starting near the top might break convention, but who cares, if it works? It enabled Cath to live her dreams. She tells me she believes you have to close one door to enable another to open. She closed the door on her career as a fabric designer by resigning without anything to go to. She took a risk, and it might not have worked, but how would she know without actually trying? "Nothing ventured, nothing gained" is surely true in this case. It is all about having courage and determination and not being afraid to lose. Great achievements are rarely gained without taking bold risks.

Cath's business is not a big corporation looking to expand and take on other photographers, but more a means of doing the work she wants to do while maintaining total control. She is not an entrepreneur or even a manager, she is a classic worker. She is the one who takes the pictures, because that's what she wants to do. The work is far more important to Cath than money. She simply will not undertake projects she doesn't like, no matter how well they pay. It is all about personal integrity and being true to oneself. Generally speaking, Cath followed her instincts, made the right choices, and took the right actions. There were times when she had some doubts about her ability to make it, but they were shortlived.

What probably made it all possible was the love of her husband, Mark, who gave her the support and confidence to step into the unknown and have a go. We all need support in one way or another, and there are dreams to be fulfilled for all of us if we are only brave enough to just have a go!

It takes courage to start a business. When starting out, you need
a deep understanding of what a business is all about and to position
yourself within the business.

CHAPTER 3:

Self-Understanding within a Business Context

THE NINE BUSINESS CONCEPTS FOR SELF-UNDERSTANDING

 These nine business concepts will help you gain self-understanding in the business context:

1. Understand the difference in founding, owning, and running businesses.

2. Understand the difference between businesses and business leaders.

3. Understand the different roles of business leaders.

4. Understand and use instruments of control.

5. Understand your motives.

6. Understand yourself.

7. Do a self-audit.

8. Balance your business and private life.

9. Embark on a journey of self-discovery and remain committed to it.

1. UNDERSTAND THE DIFFERENCE IN FOUNDING, OWNING, AND RUNNING BUSINESSES

In this book I use the term business leader generically. At one end of the spectrum is the person who starts his own business, owns it completely, and does all the work within it. At the other end of the spectrum are those people who work for others, running businesses or even business units on behalf of their employers.

There are major differences between setting up and running your own business and running businesses or business units for others. Obviously if you are running a business for someone else, you did not have to consider conceiving, founding, or setting it up. The differences are very difficult to explain properly, but

ask anyone who has set up their own business and they are likely to tell you how significant the difference is. Perhaps this is due to the degree of risk or buck stopping.

Whether you run your own business or someone else's, you may find you need to reinvent yourself every so often as the world around you changes. A reinvented business has many similarities to new businesses.

Pseudo businesses versus proper businesses

There are infinite numbers of different circumstances, which affect different people founding different businesses. I would like to draw a clear distinction particularly between those who are merely becoming self-employed, effectively doing the same thing that they were when they were employed. In this situation people may simply be changing their employed status and returning to the same company as a contractor doing exactly the same thing. In this circumstance the business is little more than an administrative convenience. This book is not primarily intended for people in these circumstances. Founding a real business is a completely different ball game. In this situation, the clear intention is to build a business rather than just create an alternative employment situation.

The litmus test

The litmus test in this circumstance is whether the business could and would survive if you, the founder, were no longer involved. If it can, you have a real business. If it can't, you are still in the self-employed stage or enroute to developing a real business.

Definitions
Founders start businesses. **Owners/Shareholders** own them. **Business** leaders run them.

2. UNDERSTAND THE DIFFERENCE BETWEEN "THE BUSINESS" AND "BUSINESS LEADERS"

One of the most important and profound messages I wish to convey is: There is a fundamental difference between the business and business leaders. It has taken me the best part of fifteen years to realize this. When I did, it literally became a life changing experience. It was as if someone had taken a foot off my head, a big cloud had lifted, and one of the great secrets of business success lay revealed. In my excitement at making this discovery, I became almost evangelical about it. The more I considered it, the more business problems were explained. If you can grasp this concept, it may well change your business and private life forever.

What happens when small new businesses are started
The best way of understanding this concept is to look at what happens when new businesses are established. Usually people are employed in someone else's business and they become dissatisfied. They want more freedom, more control and the ability to earn more money. Frequently they are the workers, the people who do the jobs. They are the auto mechanic, the hair stylist, the florist, the consultant, etc. They see that they are getting x amount of pay and their company is generating a considerably larger amount of income for the work they are doing. The logic starts with "Wouldn't it be nice if I could earn all that money

myself?" It continues, "I am the one who is doing the work," and "I got the business in the first place," and "The customer thinks I am the best person since sliced bread because I look after him so well, in fact, I am pretty invaluable around here, and all the boss does is make my life difficult, so why should I put up with this?" Or, "The boss does not know how to run his business, anyway. I could do a better job myself." It all starts here.

You start your own business in the same industry doing what you did before, only this time you are the boss. Life is great. You work extra hard because it is your business, but you do not mind because it's exciting and you enjoy doing what you are doing. Perhaps you start on your own. You are working so hard and customers think you are so good — which of course you are — that business is good. In fact, it is booming and life has never been better.

Then you come to a point when you cannot cope. There is too much work to do and you are working longer and longer hours. Day time merges to night time. Work weeks extend through the weekends until all the time you are not asleep is pretty much work time. Your health starts to suffer as do your relationships with family and friends who rarely see you and when they do, they find you tired and stressed. The consequence of not being able to cope is you start to lose control, paperwork gets left, and bills remain unpaid. Worse still, customers do not pay you money they owe you because you do not have the time to chase them. The quality of your work suffers and those once delighted customers start to complain. In your enthusiasm you may well have raised their expectations for a quality of service you are unable to deliver. Not only are you getting severe pressure from customers, but also suppliers are chasing you for payment and banks are asking you to explain why you have exceeded your loan agreement. You have become a person who is under serious pressure.

Then you have a revelation, and you realize what you need is help. If you had someone else who could do the work you did, you could take on twice the workload and, better still, pay your worker what you were paid when you were last employed, which would leave you with a big fat margin, or so you think. Being the sharp businessperson you are, you realize, too, you need someone to help you do the boring administration and accounting you so hate.

These two people arrive and life gets dramatically better. In fact, you were pretty clever to hire these people, running businesses is easy when you are as good as you are. After all, when others employed you, you thought it was easy and you could do a better job and here you are proving it. At long last you are able to reduce the number of hours you put into the business and get to enjoy life a little more. After all, you are the boss.

All goes well for a time and then, quite unexpectedly, things start to go wrong. When you are away from the business your two wonderful new employees start to change. Once they realize that you are not in the office first thing in the morning they decide that it would be okay for them to come in a little bit later, to go home a little bit earlier, to have slightly longer lunch breaks. To your amazement the quality of the work produced by your new worker is not as good as your work. You even get customer complaints about their work. You thought your accounting administration was being well managed, but to your great surprise, you find bills have been paid twice, invoices are not being generated, or invoices are calculated for the wrong amounts. If things do not change pretty quickly, you will be out of business.

These wonderful new employees, who you were so pleased to have hired in the first place, have become bad people you cannot trust, so what do you do? Of course, you know what needs to be done and you know that the only person you trust to do this properly is you. So you get right back in the business. You get involved in everything; you work harder than you have ever worked before. The result is, of course, that things do get better. By now, though, days and nights have become pretty much the same to you, you have lost your weekends, your health has started to suffer, and your private life has gone out the window again.

You are the hardest working person in your business. If you had the time to look up, what you would see is your employees watching you work. They will take their coffee breaks, lunch breaks, holidays, and go home on time while you, the business leader, will sacrifice all of yours.

At this point, perhaps your employee decides he would rather work for himself and be the boss and, worse still, he might steal your best customer. You did not think to put a restrictive covenant in his Contract of Employment to prevent him from doing just that. Alternatively, you cannot cope with doing everything yourself. Maybe you replace your employees with new employees. You see temporary improvement, but in the end, the situation reverts back to the one you previously had. Or maybe you decide to scale back your business, deciding that to employ people is too problematic.

You now realize that running a successful business is not easy and that being the boss has considerably more pressures than being the employee and that the benefits you thought you were going to get in establishing the business become a forgotten dream.

You probably think hard about what went wrong. The main reason you probably cite is that you cannot get good people, which is the bane of all businesses. At this point you are probably mentally and physically exhausted and may even feel trapped in your business. The buck stops with you, you probably have a heavy financial commitment to the business and you are quite possibly earning less than when you were employed. If you could change things you would, who wouldn't? Chances are you do not know how to change them. If you did, you would have done so already.

Release your private life from the burden of your business

The point you need to understand clearly is that, with very few exceptions, you should consider yourself and the business to be two completely different and independent things. You have created the business to work for you. You should not become a slave to the business. You are the master; the business is one of your possessions. You define, when you conceive the business, what you want it to do for you and your objective is to make sure that it does these things. You are a human being, a business is an enterprise engaged in trade. The primary purpose of the business is to serve the needs of you, its owner.

From a broader perspective, your life has a purpose and your business has a purpose. They may overlap but they are separate. Have you ever felt the pressure of your business life in your private time? Do you go to bed sometimes thinking about your business or even wake up at night thinking about it? Do you find yourself talking about your business to friends and family often?

If the answer to any of these is yes, there is a solution that can enable you to leave you business behind when you leave work. It will still be there when you go back the next day.

The solution lies in your mind. You need to be able to convince yourself that you and your business are two different things. If you are suffering the above, you can be likened to someone carrying a heavy rucksack on your back that is burdening you unnecessarily. When you finish your work for the day, mentally leave your briefcase at work; drop its weight from your shoulders. You have the right to your personal life, even if you own your own business. You also have a responsibility to yourself, your family, and friends to enjoy that private life. You can't enjoy it if it is burdened with the weight of your business worries.

Think of yourself as a doctor treating your patient, i.e., your business. You do everything in your power to ensure that your patient is fit and healthy, physically and spiritually. If your patient is healthy in all respects, you have done your job. If your patient dies despite your best efforts, you have done all you could. You haven't died, just your business. As long as you did all you could, move on and learn from the experience.

It is all down to an attitude of mind, a philosophical approach, but I promise you it works for others and for me.

....

WORDS OF WISDOM
Leave your work life when you leave the office.

....

Working on your business, not in your business

Start working "on" your business and stop working "in" it. This means you should focus your efforts on the issues that will make your business successful, namely, ensuring that your sales revenues exceed your costs and increasing shareholder value. Working in your business, you are doing the work.

Working on the business is working out what you will need to do and why, to achieve the outcomes you desire. When you work on your business, you are defining the guidelines, instructions, policies, and procedures for how everything is done in your business, and you are making sure they are adhered to.

....

WORDS OF WISDOM

Your business and your life are mutually exclusive, your business is not your life, and at most your business is simply a part of your life with its own specific purpose and values.

....

Wealth generation

With the exception of businesses started purely to provide a job, i.e., a self-employed situation, the purpose of all businesses should be to deliver shareholder value. Shareholders are the business owners. Businesses exist to create wealth for its owners, which may be derived in a number of different ways. A business may generate profit, which can be distributed to the owners as one means of wealth generation. However, adding value to the business as a whole may generate additional wealth. In practical terms this might involve the business owning assets such as machinery, property, intellectual property such as plans, designs, patents, etc., and also goodwill created through a loyal customer  base, powerful brand, booked orders, and contracted business. This value could generate wealth for the owners if they sold the business for a price greater than they had either purchased or invested into it.

3. UNDERSTAND THE DIFFERENT ROLES OF BUSINESS LEADERS

Business leaders lead other people and the business. They may be either:

- Founders/Entrepreneurs
- Owners
- Directors
- Managers
- Workers

Leadership is defined in the book, *Inspiring Leadership*, as "An influence process, working with and through others to accomplish goals of the organization."

Founders/entrepreneurs create businesses, owners own them, directors and managers run them, and workers do the work. In reality, often the same people may carry out these roles. It helps to understand, metaphorically speaking, how many hats you are wearing because there are conflicts of interest between these roles.

Business leaders carry out three key roles in differing proportions that impact the success of the business:

- Entrepreneur
- Manager
- Worker

The way they balance these three roles will be one of the greatest influencing factors in their personal fulfillment and business success.

Understanding the role of entrepreneur

Founders start businesses. They are also referred to as entrepreneurs. They may act alone or in groups. They are the people who have the ideas and motivation to start a new business. It is common practice for anyone who is starting a new business to be called an entrepreneur, which conjures up pictures of tycoons, moguls and industrialists — heroic and inspirational people creating opportunities and wealth for themselves and others. They are often portrayed as noble inventors and risk takers and are the types of people who have progressed humanity, the sort of people who have had the courage to explore an unexplored world, to put men on the moon and create the advanced world that most of us live in.

Entrepreneurs as inventors
True entrepreneurs are inventors and creators who seek possibilities in everything

under the sun. They live in the future and dream of what could be. No sooner have they created their dreams then they are looking for new challenges and opportunities, they are never, ever, satisfied. They thrive on change and competition. When they play, they play to win. Entrepreneurs typically create lots of ideas about everything under the sun. They are sometimes so far ahead that others cannot understand what they are talking about. They may be seen as impulsive, forever changing their mind and in their wake can lay a trail of chaos as their minds flit from idea to idea. They have a desire for control and can drive colleagues mad with their desire to implement change. As soon as one change has been made, another is being planned. They think so fast that others have difficulties keeping up. Without the entrepreneur there would be no new business and, indeed, established businesses would eventually go out of business.

Entrepreneurs look into the future

If one remembers that business is a voyage, a journey that never ends, the entrepreneur is looking forward to the horizon and setting the new course. Success in the business world is about the management of opportunities and threats. It is the entrepreneur who focuses on these, seizing opportunities often before others are remotely aware of them and defending against threats the others are also not aware of.

Assess your entrepreneurial rating

If there was a sliding scale for entrepreneurs from one to ten, do you know where you would fit in? Understanding your own entrepreneurial limitations is important to enable you to seek the opinions of others who are more entrepreneurial.

Understanding the role of manager

Managers manage tasks and people. They are pragmatic organizers who create order and ensure that resources, people, processes, and organization are brought together to enable corporate objectives to be achieved. If anything, they live in the past. They like structure and stability. The role of the managers is to implement the visions of the entrepreneur, although they are naturally resistant to change.

Understanding the role of worker

Workers do the work. They are interested in getting things done and they typically live in the present. They like to be in control of the work and do not like outside interference. Workers often resent managers; they dislike accountability and control, particularly relating to productivity and quality. They find it particularly difficult to understand the entrepreneur.

The three heads of the business leader

Imagine a three-headed monster in a horror film, with each head having its own agenda, but all sharing the same body. Some employees may be forgiven for seeing their business leaders as a three-headed monster. One head is the entrepreneur, one is the manager, and the last is the worker. Whenever they are talking to the business leader they never know which head they are talking to.

Internal conflicts

Imagine how difficult it is for each of the monster's heads — each wants to do different things but each shares a single body. The reality is that it is likely that each business leader in any particular set of circumstances will find that one head is the predominant one. Given that for the monster to function properly they need all three heads, it is a recipe for disaster if one or two do not have any input. Each head has its role to play to create success for the organization. The entrepreneur must set the direction and be the driving force. The manager must follow the entrepreneur's guidance and ensure the workers do the right work at the right time, to the right quality, to achieve the objective. It is a business disaster if the worker in particular, and also the manager, get to set the course and direction. Conversely, it is also a disaster if the entrepreneur has to do the work.

The problem lies in the fact that these three roles are diametrically opposed to each other and are in danger of almost continuous conflict. The fast-paced, chaotic life of the entrepreneur is at odds with the organized, structured manager, who sees problems with everything the entrepreneur is trying to achieve. The workers are at odds with the interfering manager and detest the entrepreneur, who is intent on finding interesting new work for them that they don't believe will work. A balance needs to be struck between the three, depending upon the requirements of the particular situation.

Business leader balance

Different businesses in differing circumstances will need different
proportions of entrepreneur/manager/worker attributes. The smaller the
anticipated scale of the business, the less entrepreneurial and managerial
attributes are required. The larger the scale and the greater the
ambitions, the greater the entrepreneurial and managerial attributes need
to be. Some industries are so fast-moving they need large
entrepreneurial input; others are slow-moving and require less to survive
and thrive.

Does this mean that good business leaders need to be schizophrenic?
The answer is no, they just need to be able to blend three different
attributes to meet the requirements of the circumstances. It is not
realistic to expect to be all three equally, which is what a business needs.
Entrepreneurs need to be driving the business, but managers need to be
managing it and workers need to be working. If you are a business
leader with greater manager or worker attributes, you need to develop
your entrepreneurial side. The most effective business leaders work on
the business, not in it. Workers or managers should not be leading
businesses.

Different people, different perspectives

The obvious solution is to have a team of business leaders with
complimentary strengths and weaknesses, who all recognize the real
needs of the business. In practice, however, this is an ideal that is very
difficult to achieve for a whole variety of different reasons including
cost and mutual understanding. In any situation it is common for
different people to have different perspectives and understanding. This is
one of the factors that makes creating a successful business so difficult.

*"To the Manager, the Technician (Worker) becomes a problem to
be managed. To the Technician (Worker) the Manager becomes a
meddler to be avoided. To both of them the Entrepreneur is the
one who got them into trouble in the first place."*
— Michael Gerber, author, The E-Myth Revisited

4. UNDERSTAND AND USE INSTRUMENTS OF CONTROL

The success of any business and personal fulfillment of its leaders is inextricably linked to the choices and actions made by its founders and business leaders. They are ultimately accountable for the success or failure of the business and for their own personal fulfillment, for they carry the burden of making those choices and ensuring the implementation of chosen actions.

The secret of business success is to make the right choices and successfully implement the right actions. This sounds blindingly obvious, but it is easier said than done.

Business failure is a result of:

- Wrong choices
- Right choices, but failing on their implementation
- Ignorance, therefore making no choices and taking no action

The role of a business leader is extremely important to the success of any business. The role is difficult to quantify and accurately define. There are few sources of reference that take a holistic view of the business leader's roles. The difficulty is that there are an infinite set of different circumstances and issues. Leadership is the most important element of their role.

Business leaders, by definition, lead businesses. Business leaders are "the boss," they make choices; they initiate actions and measure and analyze the results, making new choices and initiating new actions. They have responsibilities to themselves and others, which is a burden.

Understanding this is the easy part, doing something about it and becoming a good business leader is harder. How do you separate your business and private lives? How do you start to work on your business and not in it? How do you end up with outcomes different from those described? How can you practically treat you and your business as two entirely separate things?

There are two sides to this issue: one is yourself and the other is your business. You need to gain a better self-understanding first and then understand how better to manage the relationship between your work and private life. Later in the book, I will tell you in more detail how to work on your business and not in it .

Choices

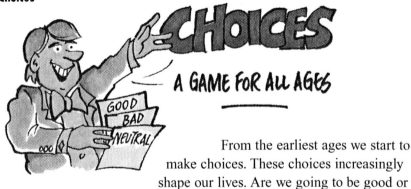

From the earliest ages we start to make choices. These choices increasingly shape our lives. Are we going to be good or bad, are we going to work at school or not. What job do we want to do, where do we want to live, whose company do we want to keep etc.

There are just three key choices:

1. Good Choices
2. Bad Choices
3. Neutral Choices

It is only after they have been made that we know whether they were good, bad, or neutral. It is also down to personal opinion as to what is good, bad, or neutral.

Having made a choice, we have another one to decide and that is whether there is anything we can learn from the choices we made and the outcomes we experienced.

Choices are phenomenally significant in life, yet are rarely discussed. Choices can bring us happiness or sadness, poverty or wealth, life or death. I suggest that by giving more attention to choices in a personal and business context that desired outcomes can be greatly improved.

How to make good choices

- Pause to consider alternatives.

- Review all alternatives and attempt to make objective judgments.

- Consider opinions of others.

....

WORDS OF WISDOM

Never let bad choices spoil your future.

You can't change the past, so don't beat yourself up over it; you can change the future though.

....

Actions

Choices and decisions are totally useless unless they are followed up with the corresponding action. For example, at a board meeting the members decide to invest in an advertising program to generate new business. They have clearly made the choice to invest in advertising; they have, after all, documented it in the board minutes. Unless someone takes some action to put together the program, book the advertising space, and make sure it happens, nothing will happen.

Actions are the fulfillment of choices. By necessity there is always going to be a time delay between a choice being made and the action being taken. The time delay is critical. It is too late to start the advertising campaign when you have run out of money because you had no sales. Advertising too early, before you have products to sell can be a waste of time if customers go elsewhere.

What type of actions do you take? Is your timing mostly right? Are your choices and actions in sync? Do you make too many involuntary actions? Can you understand the need to balance choices with actions? Are your choices realistic?

How do you relate to others regarding choices and actions? Do you mostly make the choices and complete the actions yourself or do you make the choices and others complete them?

We all share the world with others; in our private and work lives we interact with others. We continually make choices and take actions and also follow actions that are initiated by the choices of others. How we manage these can affect our personal and professional success.

Actions can be categorized into two areas:

- Voluntary
- Involuntary

Voluntary actions

Voluntary actions are the result of choices. They result from conscious decisions to do something. Involuntary actions are those you didn't intend to do, e.g., crashing your car, spilling your coffee over your work.

Involuntary actions

Involuntary actions can be further divided into two categories:

Innocent: Could not have been prevented by person making action.

Culpable: Could have been prevented by person making action.

An innocent involuntary action is when the action you take is not consciously planned, but results from external circumstances beyond your control, e.g., someone bumps into you and makes you spill your coffee. Culpable involuntary action is when you become distracted, trip, and spill your coffee. Had you been watching where you were going, the action could have been prevented.

Measurement and analysis

Actions will result in outcomes. Was the outcome more than you desired and expected or less? You will only know by making sure that you know what the outcome was and comparing it to what you expected and desired.

By measuring and analyzing the outcomes you can continue to do the things that work and stop or change doing the things that don't.

Responsibility

With choices and actions come responsibilities to others and us. We might choose to drive our car fast, but doing so might put the lives of others in danger. If we injure someone as a result, we are responsible for our choices and actions and we have to suffer the consequences.

As business owners, we have responsibilities to our customers, suppliers, and employees. We have responsibilities to the environment, our neighbors, governments, and others. We are responsible for the success or failure of our business.

Accountability

With responsibilities come accountabilities. We make choices, which initiate actions, which deliver outcomes. We are responsible for the outcomes as they resulted from our actions; at the least we are accountable to ourselves, but often to others as well.

Using your instruments of control

Awareness of your instruments of control should enable you to see why you might have lost control in the past and why you might feel like too much of your personal and business life outcomes are outside your control.

Work on improving your decision making, and make a habit of learning from your experiences. It is unforgivable to keep making the same mistakes.

....

WORDS OF WISDOM

To manage people, business and your life, think, act, assess and analyze outcomes, then think more and act again.

Measure twice, cut once.

Always learn from your experiences whether good or bad.

....

5. UNDERSTAND YOUR MOTIVES

There are reasons why we do things or do not do things and also why things happen or do not happen. What we achieve in our business and private lives is partly influenced by circumstances outside our control and partly by our own choices and actions.

What prompts us to make any choice or take any action? Whatever this is, this is our motive, our reason for doing or not doing something. The chances are that you have not thought too much about why you do things. It is as if we all have an in-built autopilot that sets us on the path of convention. Perhaps this exercise will give you a new insight into yourself and enable you to focus more on what you are trying to achieve: try to question and understand why you have done things in the past; this will help you question and review your motives for doing things in the future.

6. UNDERSTAND YOURSELF

Business leaders create and run businesses. First and foremost they are people with hopes, dreams and aspirations just like other people. Business leaders are not superior people; they are just people whose chosen role is leadership. They could just as easily choose to be teachers, doctors, nurses, road sweepers, or toilet cleaners.

If you were to take all the packaging off any business, you would see that at its core are people. People create businesses, people run businesses, people support businesses, and behind every customer are more people.

To run a successful business, business leaders, need to firstly understand themselves and then understand others.

The difficulty in gaining self-understanding

It is more difficult to understand people than you might expect. Arguably, you know yourself better than anyone else, you have been yourself since the day you were conceived, you know everything about yourself, where you have been, what you have done, etc. Do you know what you are capable of achieving? Could you run a mile in under four minutes? Could you run into a burning building, risking your own life to save others? Could you cope being on a plane that crashed in the middle of the Amazon rain forest? Could you turn your tiny business into a multi–billion-dollar global enterprise? Could you make a difference in someone's life?

The truth is you can't know for sure unless you try. There is a big difference between what you think you can do and what you can actually do. In some cases, you would be surprised at what you could achieve and perhaps you would be even more surprised about what you couldn't achieve. We all hold perceptions about ourselves. These perceptions influence our beliefs about our capabilities and aspirations.

WORDS OF WISDOM

Business is all about people.

Perceptions can hold you back or help you succeed; from time to time you need to challenge them.

See yourself as others see you

I get my hair cut once every six to eight weeks. Each time the barber holds up the mirror to show me the haircut, I see a little gray patch of hair on the side of my head. This is the only time I see it, yet others I don't know very well get to see it every day. If the barber hadn't held up the mirror, I would never have known about it. It is hardly important, but it illustrates a point.

It is easy to think you know yourself, but it is difficult to see yourself, not just physically looking in a mirror, but metaphorically too. You are often too close to see yourself as others see you. Another example is when you hear your own voice on a tape recorder; you don't sound the same as you think you sound when you are speaking. Like having a magnifying glass too close, everything is distorted and out of focus, yet looking from a distance, everything is crystal clear.

The path to better self-understanding

To gain a better self-understanding consider the following aspects about yourself:

- Personality
- Skills
- Experience
- Knowledge

Who are you?

In trying to better understand yourself, you have to consider there are three of you as follows:

1. Who you think you are
2. Who others think you are
3. Who you truly are

We all hold perceptions about ourselves. Others, too, will hold perceptions about us based on their experiences and judgments of us. These perceptions may be similar or different. Yet if one were able to make a totally impartial judgment representing the truth, the results might again be similar or different. Which matters most? I am concerned about what others think, but I use my own judgments and values to lead my life and I am continually driven to find the truth, the real me. Understanding your own strengths and weaknesses, preferences and attributes is fundamental to the success you are looking for your business to achieve.

Understanding your knowledge, experience and skills in most areas is relatively easy, e.g., generic business knowledge, market knowledge, industry knowledge, etc. To become an accountant or an attorney, you study, take examinations, and are awarded recognized qualifications. Professional rules, standards, and laws govern the work you do.

Arguably, these could qualify you to be in business in these fields, yet these qualifications say very little about your ability to run an accounting or law business. It is often the most important areas that are most difficult to define.

How do you judge your entrepreneurial, managerial, or worker skills? Because these issues are hard to define, they are often ignored. There are few assessments, training courses, or sources of information specifically tailored to the particular requirements of business leadership. It is very much an untouched or, at best, lightly touched area because it is a very difficult one to address. I have been on the journey of conscious self-discovery for a very long time and have only just unlocked the answers that I have been seeking for so long.

If you are looking to understand these issues yourself, I can help show you the way. Ultimately, it is a journey of self-discovery that never totally ends and one that only you can take. To take it you have to have the desire and interest. As with most things in life, everyone's journey to self-discovery will be different. There are an infinite number of paths to take. The starting point should be to understand your own personality.

Who would you like to be?

 In just the same way it is important to consider who you are, your true self, it is also important to visualize yourself from the perspectives of:

- The person you present to the world.

- The person you would like to be.

- The person you need to be.

Personality secrets revealed

Personality theory dates back to the fifth century B.C. when Hippocrates defined four distinct energies that relate to different people. Since that time psychologists have developed an advanced understanding of personality and preferences. While we are all unique human beings with our own interests, motivations, and personalities, we can be categorized into personality types, which offer considerable insights into our personalities and the things that make us tick. In particular, personality testing can identify the following:

- Personal style
- Understanding of how we interact with others
- Understanding of how we make decisions
- Strengths
- Weaknesses
- The value that we bring to a team
- How other people should best communicate with us
- How other people should not attempt to communicate with us
- Our blind spots
- Our opposite types and how we should deal with them and they with us
- Our ideal work environment
- How we can best be managed
- What motivates us
- How we manage others
- Our life purpose
- How to manage time and life
- How to manage personal creativity
- How we can best learn
- Our attitude/orientation preferences
- Our rational (judging) functions
- Our irrational (perceiving) functions

The jigsaw puzzle of self-enlightenment

Gaining self-understanding is like doing a jigsaw puzzle. You start with some pieces and try to put them together. Sometimes the different pieces of the jigsaw look inconsistent with each other and it is difficult to see that they can belong together. If you are able to put enough pieces of the jigsaw puzzle together you begin to see the picture. The more you put together, the more of the picture you can see, until the point at which you can see everything, even if there are a few holes remaining.

There are various stages in your life when you re-assess your priorities and search for happiness and fulfillment by looking inward rather than just outward. I have to warn you, you might not always like what you see when you look inward. Remember, while you cannot change the past, you can change the future. What you have done and what you were is history. You have the ability to make choices and define actions that you wish to make in the future.

If you continue doing what you have always done, the likelihood is you will continue to get the same results. If you are looking to change your life for the better and to improve your business success, make a positive choice to do so, and embark upon a new journey where you leave your past behind.

7. DO A SELF-AUDIT

If you have made a conscious decision to embark upon a new voyage of self-discovery or to continue an existing one, the first step is to do a self-audit by going through a process which enables you to work out, firstly, where your sources of reference are and, secondly, what knowledge you currently have available.

The most difficult to overcome is that of personal bias. You need to be prepared to question your own perceptions about yourself, which is something that is very difficult to do.

How easy you find this will depend on your personality type. For some it is an impossible task.

You have to be committed to objectivity and discovering the truth, however unpalatable it may prove to be. As human beings, we are all full of failings, we have all done things that we have subsequently regretted and we all have egos, some stronger than others!

To complete a self-audit you need to be prepared to seek knowledge and information, write it down, sort it, and analyze it.

You can complete a self-audit at: **www.thebusinessvoyage.com/bv/selfaudit.html**

WORDS OF WISDOM
With any negative, there is always a positive, if you look for it. With any failure, there is an opportunity to learn and develop.

Sources of reference
To understand yourself, use every available source of knowledge and information and leave no stone unturned. Some of the possible sources of information are:

- Yourself
- Your family
- Friends
- Work colleagues
- Your suppliers

- Your customers
- Previous work appraisals
- Previous training courses/assessments and notes

Information about yourself

Auditing yourself is all about gaining knowledge about you. Once you have done this, you need to categorize the information into four groups:

❏ Knowledge and perceptions obtained from yourself

❏ Knowledge and perceptions obtained from others

❏ Knowledge and perceptions that you have proof are true

❏ Knowledge gained from personality and other assessments

The knowledge and information you require can be categorized into the following four groups:

- **Personality:** What are you like?
- **Skills:** What can you do?
- **Experience:** What have you done?
- **Knowledge:** What do you know?

How to understand your personality

The personality, information, and knowledge are the most difficult to capture and by far the most valuable. Your personal success and business success is inextricably linked to your knowledge of your personality. With good knowledge of your personality you can capitalize on your strengths, compensate for your weaknesses, and understand why you have the impact that you do on your business and the people around you. You cannot change your personality but you can change some of the actions that you take and the situations you place yourself in. For example, if you are not a good manager, understand why you are not a good manager and identify what actions you need to take to meet the needs of those you are managing or, alternatively, recognize that management is not your best skill and allow others who are exceptional managers to do the managing.

After considerable searching, I have found a personality testing tool I feel stands head and shoulders above any others I have seen or used.

To find details of how you can use this emal: **enquiry @asapinstitute.com** (Costs approx. £120)

After you complete a simple exercise that takes approximately twenty minutes, we will be able to generate a forty-page report which includes the following:

Personality test

- ❏ Introduction
- ❏ Overview
  - Personal Style
  - Interacting with Others
  - Decision Making
- ❏ Key Strengths and Weaknesses
  - Strengths
  - Possible Weaknesses
- ❏ Value to the Team
- ❏ Communication
  - Effective Communications
  - Barriers to Effective Communication
- ❏ Possible Blind Spots
- ❏ Difficult Person
  - Communication with Your Difficult Person
- ❏ Suggestions for Development
- ❏ Management
  - Creating the Ideal Environment
  - Managing You
  - Motivating You
- ❏ Management Style
- ❏ Effective Selling Chapter
- ❏ Selling Style Overview
- ❏ Before the Sale Begins
- ❏ Identifying Needs
- ❏ Proposing
- ❏ Handling Buying Resistance

- ❏ Gaining Commitment
- ❏ Follow-up and Follow-through
- ❏ Sales Preference Indicators
- ❏ Personal Achievement Chapter
- ❏ Living on Purpose
- ❏ Time and Life Management
- ❏ Personal Creativity
- ❏ Lifelong Learning
- ❏ Learning Styles
- ❏ Interview Questions
- ❏ The Insights Wheel
- ❏ Insights Color Dynamics
- ❏ Jungian Preferences

8. BALANCE YOUR BUSINESS AND PRIVATE LIFE

We all come into this world alone and we finally leave alone. In between is our life, our time on earth. None of us knows how much time we have, whether we will live to a ripe old age or suffer an early death through illness, accident, or misfortune.

As children, we have little comprehension about the finality of our lives; we live in the present, look forward to the immediate future perhaps, but have little thought for what lies ahead.

Managing time

A morbid thought perhaps to what I hope is an inspiring and uplifting book, which may change some people's lives forever. Time is the thread that makes up our lives. What matters is what we do with that time, which is one of the main themes of this book. Life is a journey, full of twists and turns, ups and downs that we share with others. We can influence our life journey, but we also have to accept that it will be influenced for us by others or circumstances beyond our control.

Making choices

In adulthood, we have our working lives and our private lives, running in parallel but intertwined. While at work, our thoughts and actions are often private and personal ones, whether it be socializing with work colleagues or planning your vacation. Equally, on weekends and in the evening, we can often think of work problems and issues or even take work home to do. Getting the balance right between these is difficult for most people. We are conditioned by the environment and others around us to accept the status quo; we often forget that we have choices. Many people are frightened about making choices; they want others to make the choices for them. With choices comes responsibility and accountability to others and to us.

Understanding the relationship between private and work lives

In trying to understand the relationship between our work and private lives, we need to consider the impact on our families and friends. It is also important we understand our employees and colleagues' relationships between their private and work lives and help them find an acceptable balance between the two.

WORDS OF WISDOM
Life is not a rehearsal – live it to the full while you can.

Segmenting our lives

Our lifetime can be segmented in many different ways:

How we pass our time

Awake two thirds	Asleep one third
Happy	Neutral
Listening	Silent
Thinking	Observing
Excited	Indifferent
Giving	Passive, etc.
Sad	
Speaking	
Feeling	
Bored	
Receiving	

The important question regarding the way we segment our lives is what is important to us. Whatever we decide we like to do or experience, we can make choices and take actions that increase our chances of achieving our goals. What gives us happiness?

WORDS OF WISDOM

There are just three things that make you happy:

1. Having something to look forward to

2. Making other people happy

3. Sharing

Without making choices and taking action, things are likely to stay the same.

Stages of life

We all go through various stages in our lives, during which our priorities, desires, attitudes, and motivations change. If we recognize the transition from one stage to another and look to positively manage it, we stand more chance of achieving fulfillment. Examples of some life stages are as follows:

Career Stages	Educating	Working	Retired
Dependency Stages	Dependent	Independent	Dependent
Marital Stages	Single	Married	Widowed

Planning your life and changing your future

What would you do if you knew you only had six months to live? It doesn't matter if it is a day, a week, a month, a year, or more. The issue is that this question makes you think about what is most important to you. It is remarkable how few people actually take the trouble to think this through. It is a difficult question to answer, perhaps, but if you have the misfortune to be told you have just six months to live, I promise you it will make you think very hard.

You don't need something bad to happen to make you reassess your life, so do it frequently. Your choices are:

- Carry on doing what you are currently doing.
- Change what you are currently doing.
- Do something completely different.

Look after yourself

If you don't look after yourself, the chances are nobody else will. On our journey of life and business voyages we all need to look after ourselves, mentally and physically.

Leading any business has its challenges and stresses and it will take its toll unless you actually take positive action to prevent it. Running businesses takes considerable time and energy. Given that we have a finite amount of both, giving too much to our business can mean that other parts of our life suffer.

After three years of running a PLC, I saw my weight increase, level of fitness and overall health decline. The reason being, I was working too hard to look after myself. Has this happened to you?

It takes willpower and a conscious effort to do something about it. In my case I contacted a firm of fitness consultants and now spend three hours a week with a personal trainer and many more hours with my young children doing energetic things. Surprise, surprise, I have lost weight, become much fitter, and feel considerably better.

Look after your loved ones

We hear too often of children growing up hardly knowing their parents because their parents are too busy working. Once a childhood is gone, it can't be recovered. Marriages will only work well if they are cherished. What is the point in having a successful business and a shattered family?

Regret is no good after the event. Don't lose, through blindness, the things that are most valuable to you.

9. EMBARK ON A JOURNEY OF SELF-DISCOVERY AND REMAIN COMMITTED TO IT

Self-understanding not only helps you define and achieve your objectives, but also greatly increases the chances of achieving happiness and fulfillment.

You might well go through a process of self-discovery, which will give you a snapshot of where you are at the current time. As you progress through life you will change, as will the circumstances you face. Can you imagine if you were to run your life based on the you of yesterday rather than on the you of today? It might not work as well as you would like it to. Your motives and objectives will change, so too should your choices and actions to reflect the new circumstances.

Daily questions

Ask yourself these two questions every day:

1. Who am I?
2. What do I want?

Spiritual enlightenment

For some this topic is easy to laugh off, but if you have enough questions you will realize that this is the path to take and it will bring rewards. Your personal and business success is all wrapped up in you, the business leader and your willingness to explore other avenues.

One of the greatest successes man can achieve is inner contentment. The world is full of supposedly successful people who have made it, with riches beyond most people's wildest dreams, and recognition and adoration from the world at large, but they are often spiritually empty, insecure, and unhappy. Pop stars, models, and top businessmen face many of the same issues — the newspapers are full of stories about their breakdowns, alcohol or drug abuse, or the demise of their relationships. Perhaps it is a case of the higher you are, the further you have to fall.

Spiritual enlightenment is a greater awareness and understanding of yourself and your behavior. It is a journey that never ends. You might continually learn more, but there is always more to learn.

Emotional intelligence

The term, emotional intelligence, was adopted by Peter Salovey and Jack Meyer in 1990 and was used to describe the way people bring intelligence to their emotions to create success. This represents qualities other than IQ that are materialized in terms of behavior.

To understand how you use emotional intelligence to influence your success, open your mind to greater self-understanding and understanding of how you can combine management skills, leadership attributes, and personal attributes to achieve results through effective and inspiring leadership.

Imagine if it were possible to observe people in laboratory-controlled conditions, living and working together where every decision, action, and result is recorded in both the work and social environment? What might one be able to learn? Reality TV programs such as "Big Brother," where participants are locked up in a house with TV cameras and microphones able to record everything, twenty-four hours a day, can give some insight into what might happen, but these shows are intended for entertainment, not academic purposes.

Imagine if it were possible to run twelve identical experiments over an extended period of time with, say, eighteen people in each experiment — an impossible prospect perhaps? Between 2000 and 2001 it actually happened, and it was possible to study how emotional intelligence works in practice and influences performance.

The concept was a stroke of genius. Twelve identical yachts were taking part in the world's toughest yacht race, the BT Global Challenge. Each identical yacht had a skipper and seventeen randomly placed crew members. The whole event was used as a structured research project managed by a distinguished team: Jane Cranwell-Ward, Andrea Bacon, and Rosie Mackie. Thousands of interviews with skippers and crews were carried out after every leg of the grueling race and the results assimilated and analyzed. They concluded: "The race was highly competitive, the environment hostile, at times dangerous, and conditions were uncertain. Faced with these pressures and racing identical yachts, the winners were the skippers who led their teams most effectively to achieve and sustain high performance."

This race provides a great parallel with the modern business world and supports the nautical analogies used in this book. This research conclusively proves the power of emotional intelligence.

Take charge of your life, don't let your life take charge of you

Sometimes you need to take a step back and reassess where you are going, what you are doing and what you are hoping to achieve. Do you want to be fulfilled and happy? Of course you do, but how far are you prepared to go to achieve it? Are you willing to take the time to give the issue some thought and then actually do something about it?

When was the last time you went for a thorough health checkup? Do you spend more money servicing your car than you do yourself? Are you spending enough time with your family? Are your children growing up fast, should you be making the most of the time that they want to be with you? Are you giving them enough of your time? Is there anything you would truly like to do, and is there anything stopping you from doing it? Is there anywhere you want to go, anything you want to experience? Have you seen the sunrise in the Sahara, the glow of the Aurora Borealis, or the tropical paradise of French Polynesia?

....

WORDS OF WISDOM

Be bold and brave, make some decisions and act while you still can. You have to assume that you only have one life. Endeavor to make the most of it.

....

Bring back time management

If you were in business in the eighties, you will remember the age of the Filofax, when time management was the latest concept and young urban professionals were Yuppies. Whatever has happened to time management as a concept? I think it is about time we brought it back and dusted it off.

Have you noticed we have more time management technology than we have ever had in the history of mankind, and time management is a bigger issue than it has ever been in the past? Personal organizers and electronic diary systems are everywhere, but there is still never enough time and we still waste far too much of what we do have. It is such a valuable commodity; we must learn to value it. Our bank account of time is only going down!

There is nothing wrong with the technology tools available to help us manage our time. It is how we use them, or don't use them, that is the issue. Many of us will happily spend several hundred dollars buying the technology, but very few people would consider spending the same amount on learning the techniques and skills of time management. Time management isn't rocket science, it is basic common sense, but when you are too close or too busy, you become caught in a catch-22 situation where you don't have time to address the issue that, if addressed, would give you the time to do so.

REAL-LIFE STORY
My dear father-in-law died a few years back of prostate cancer at the age of fifty-seven. He was a dairy farmer in the United Kingdom. Farming was all he had ever known; he was brought up on a farm where he no doubt worked as a child. He took on a farm of his own in his early twenties. He worked hard, seven days a week, from early in the morning to late at night, and often through the night. He had four wonderful children with his wife who also worked hard on the farm. They planned for retirement and designed and built their dream home on some of their land, but he died before the house was finished and he had the chance to fulfill his retirement dreams. His perspective on life changed when he was diagnosed with cancer. He realized even more than ever how important his family was, and he made sure he let them know how much he loved them. Fortunately, he said if he could live his life again he wouldn't change a thing.

REAL-LIFE STORY
In 1990 at the age of twenty-six, I was taking part in the Two-handed Transatlantic Yacht Race from Plymouth in the United Kingdom to Newport, Rhode Island in the United States. Halfway across the ocean, the yacht started to fall apart and the crew headed back toward Ireland, the nearest land. The situation deteriorated further when a severe storm, mountainous seas, and a major leak were topped with failed steering that left the yacht drifting helplessly in deep water. A daring, record-breaking rescue by the Royal Air Force resulted in the crew being airlifted off the

yacht some three hundred miles west of Ireland with just minutes to spare. Did that change my life? It certainly did. It made me appreciate my family more and made me want to live my life to the fullest.

We all experience life-altering moments such as the loss of someone we know, the arrival of a new baby, losing our jobs, experiencing a health scare, surviving a significant event such as 9/11, or simply realizing we are getting older, a midlife crisis. How often do people wish they had changed their lives sooner? Quite often, I suspect.

To adventure is to undertake a venture of uncertain outcomes, an exciting experience that is likely to involve risks and dangers. People who set up businesses are adventurers in every sense. It is not for everyone, but if it is for you, hold your head high and bravely set off on your own adventure. Good luck and remember that every adventure starts with good planning and preparation.

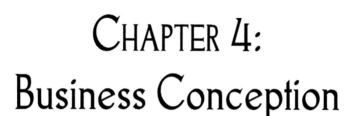

CHAPTER 4:

Business Conception

BUSINESS CONCEPTION INTRODUCTION

Businesses don't just happen. People or groups of people who are driven by ideas and dreams conceive them.

Anyone can conceive a business, from any background, education, age, or experience. Conceiving a business is a conscious act that is driven by two key components — motivation and ideas. People who conceive businesses and bring them into existence are  called entrepreneurs. Entrepreneurs create opportunities and wealth for themselves and others. They are the backbone of capitalist society.

> *"Life hangs on a very thin thread and the cancer of time is complacency. If you are going to do something, do it now. Tomorrow is too late."* — Pete Goss

Motivation

Motivation is simply something that prompts a person to take action. Our own personal influences motivate us. Two key elements comprise our personal influences:

- Circumstances beyond our control
- Personal choices

We'll now look at some key motivators that prompt people to conceive businesses.

Money

Businesses exist for the benefit of shareholders, i.e., owners. Shareholders invest in businesses to obtain shareholder value, which is quantified by return on investments. Owning equity in businesses provides opportunities for wealth generation beyond people's wildest expectations. It also provides risk of wealth loss. Business ownership is often driven by greed, where the perceived opportunity makes the risks worthwhile. In stock markets, shareholders will sell when they perceive, i.e., when they fear, their equity value is threatened.

When somebody establishes a business, they become its shareholder, but they usually also derive income in terms of salary or a draw. In most businesses the higher up the management tree you are, the greater the earnings you receive. Obviously, as a business owner, you can decide how much to pay yourself within the constraints of the business, a very attractive proposition for most people.

Money doesn't buy happiness, but it does provide security. We all need money to fund our lifestyles and pay for the basics of food, clothing, and shelter.

Satisfaction

Creating a business can be extremely rewarding. It can afford business owners a feeling of great achievement and pride.

Power

Becoming the boss puts you in authority and enables you to make the choices and take the actions you desire. This can be a very liberating experience.

Freedom and control

Setting your own working hours, choosing your work location, and creating your own work environment to suit your interests and tastes can provide a stark contrast to the employed environment where these factors are normally outside your control. With control, however, come responsibilities. Owning and running your own company may seem idealistic at the start and some people may by disappointed to find themselves with less freedom, time, and control than they previously had. The buck stops with you.

Challenge

The advancement of mankind is driven by the need to create challenges, to push back the limits, to do things that have never been done before. It is this love of challenge that has driven man to go to the moon, people to climb Everest, and sportsmen to set new world records. Most people in life are followers; entrepreneurs tend to be pioneers and explorers, continually advancing.

Necessity

If you can't find employment, there is often little choice other than to start your own business. An example of this might be people who are down-and-out, who have lost their way in life, and who earn money any way they can, even by begging, with no clear plan for the future.

Ideas

If motivation is something that prompts people to take action, the ideas are the actions themselves.

YOUR BUSINESS CHOICES

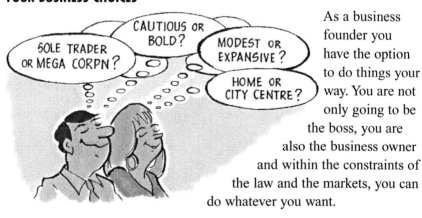

As a business founder you have the option to do things your way. You are not only going to be the boss, you are also the business owner and within the constraints of the law and the markets, you can do whatever you want.

What do you want to do?

What industry do you want to be in? Do you want to be a hair stylist, boat builder, consultant? The choice is yours.

How do you want to do it?

Do you want to be big or small? Do you want to work from home? Do you want to be Internet-based? Do you want a few or lots of employees? Do you want to be bold and expansive? Do you want to be cautious or modest? What name do you want? Where do you want to operate?

Why should customers buy from you?

All businesses need customers to enable them to generate sales revenues, which, ideally, produce profits. Is there a demand for the products and services you wish to sell, or can you create them? Why should potential customers buy from you and not somebody else? Are you going to be unique selling things that others can't, perhaps inventing your own products or services, or will you be located in a place convenient to customers? Are you going to be cheaper, or is your quality of service going to be better, or both? You might choose to start a business, but customers will decide whether you remain in business. Businesses can't exist without sales revenue.

Businesses exist to meet the needs of their shareholders. From the business' perspective, customers are there to enable them to achieve their objectives. From the customers' perspective, they purchase from suppliers to meet their objectives. The secret is to create a win-win situation for all concerned. A win-lose or lose-win situation is unsustainable.

THE PROCESS OF BUSINESS CONCEPTION

Businesses are conceived in many different ways. At one extreme, a big bang, a sudden realization, a bolt from the blue, a magic moment, an overnight dream and at the other, a nucleus, the tiniest

germ of an idea, forming an essential element of the concept growth, perhaps materialized in the subconscious initially until large enough to be noticed by the conscious mind.

To conceive a business, you often need a catalyst. This could be a life-changing event that makes you reconsider your life direction or, perhaps, a circumstantial event such as losing your job or someone else suggesting you start a business. The starting point is either motivation or ideas.

If motivation is an egg and the idea is a sperm, the business can't take life unless the egg is fertilized. In other words, there can't be life without the two being brought together in perfect harmony.

Whatever the start, business conception is a process and not just a one-time event. The egg has to take root and develop into an embryo. To do so, it needs mental energy, commitment, and the right environment. If motivation is insufficient, the business concept will not be brought to reality. The process of business conception takes place in the minds of its founders.

From conception to reality

The point at which a business concept turns to reality we call the "reality point." Once this stage is passed, the founders start to lay the foundations for the business where investment is made and the risks start. This is the setup phase, which must be undertaken before a business can start to trade.

If we imagine a business as a boat, the founder has decided he wants one, he knows what he wants it for, and he has the motivation to create it. At this point, the metaphoric business is conceived. To bring the concept to reality, the motivation needs to remain and the details thought through. If the motivation dwindles and sufficient details are not thought through, the boat will never be created and the business concept will die. If there is sufficient detail and motivation, the founder will commission the naval architects and engineers to prepare the necessary plans. This is the setup point at which investment is made to pay the naval architects and engineers and, therefore, risks are taken. At this point, there is no guarantee that either the boat will be built or that its building will deliver the outcomes its founder anticipated. At any stage prior to the boat's launch, the project could fail and the boat/business will never, metaphorically speaking, come to life.

Risks invariably precede rewards. The future will always be uncertain and nothing can be totally guaranteed.

Aspirations

Different founders will have different aspirations and different plans. The bigger and more ambitious the plans, the greater the potential benefits, but also the greater the potential risks. Conversely, small plans and low aspirations potentially offer lower risks and lower benefits. One of the first choices any business founder has to make is to decide the scale of his or her potential business operation.

When the U.K. mobile phone company, Orange, was founded, the aspirations of its founders were huge. They raised hundreds of millions of pounds with the full knowledge it would take years before they reached profitability. At the other end of the spectrum is the one-man business, where an IT consultant decides to become an independent contractor and the business is little short of a temporary employment situation. There are no hard and fast rules about what size a new business should be.

Founder reality check

Whenever anyone thinks about setting up a business, they invariably think of the positives, the up sides, and the potential. The ideas and the expectations create excitement, enthusiasm, and adrenaline rushes. These are all essential ingredients needed to create businesses.

Few people think too much about the risks, the downsides and the negatives. Those setting up businesses for the first time are like newborn children, experiencing a new world for the very first time.

With no guardians to protect them, newborn business people will often learn the hard way, suffering injuries as a result of walking into dangers without knowing what dangers lay before them. Even when they are injured for the first time, they sometimes don't realize why and subsequently keep making the same mistakes.

It is possible the business founders won't achieve any of the things that made them establish the business in the first place such as money, satisfaction, power, challenge, freedom, control, etc.

Furthermore, they might lose everything they have worked so hard to achieve in their lives to date such as wealth, happiness, health, and security. Most business founders think it won't happen to them, just like some young people who have unprotected sex and don't think they are at risk for catching HIV.

New business founders are very similar to young people growing up — enthusiastic risk-takers sometimes over-confident about their own abilities. One has to remember that maturity and experience in a private life is separate from maturity and experience in a business life. People working for others in a business, even in senior managerial positions, will find the experience of creating and running their own business very different. This is difficult to comprehend until you have experienced it first hand. No amount of book reading or studying can adequately prepare you. The only way a child will learn to walk is to try, fall down, get up and try again.

To be forewarned and prepared is a great advantage, but success and survival rely on the judgment and preparations of the founders and their ability to learn from their mistakes.

The importance of support

New business founders should seek the support of anyone who can help them. There are four key areas of support:

1. Professionals
2. Experienced and successful business founders
3. Friends and family
4. Business advisers

Professionals are solicitors and accountants who are bound by professional codes of conduct. While these professionals may be able to

offer valuable commercial advice, their main purpose is to enable businesses to comply with laws and standards that govern business.

People who have founded successful businesses are the people most likely to understand the issues that new business founders will face; they will have learned the hard way. The only way to know what it is like to be a parent is to be one.

Moral support from those you care about and who care about you is important to support you through the inevitable tough times. You will want these people to share the joys of successes with you as well. As we have all heard many times, "A trouble shared is a trouble halved."

There are usually many business advisers available should you look for them. Some will provide their advice for free and others for a fee. These advisers might include:

- Bankers
- Government bodies
- Business consultants
- Trade organizations

Self-belief and determination

Belief and determination are the two things that will enable you to bring your business conception to reality. The selling starts with you. You have got to believe that the business concept is right and that you have the ability to make it successful and deliver the outcomes you desire.

You need time to consider all the issues and weigh up in your own mind the risk versus reward. Visualize the steps you will need to take to create and run your business. Can you see yourself taking on the responsibilities, standing accountable for your own actions and casting off the securities of salaried employment?

You might start with broad-brush thoughts of the bigger issues, the more you think about it, and the more you think about the details, the practicalities and the realities. From thoughts you will develop plans and make assumptions and you will start to write down your thoughts, which will give the first sense of reality to your proposed business.

If you are lucky, your conviction will be so strong that you will have no doubts and will be fully committed. In most situations however, most business founders will at sometime experience moments of doubt, which will affect their determination. This is not uncommon and is actually a positive process, which enables you to test your concepts mentally without committing to them or taking risks. It's much better to "measure twice, cut only once."

Passion

Are you passionate about your business? Does your business inspire emotions within you of pride, absolute confidence, enthusiasm, and conviction? It can help, particularly in a sales situation. Your enthusiasm, excitement and self-belief are contagious for both employees and customers.

Being passionate about your business is one of the best motivators there is. The danger for the business is that the passion lives in you, and is only passed to the business when you are there. The longer you are established the harder it is to maintain that passion. Problems and people can wear you down; you may feel ill, tired or stressed and your perspective changes.

You will be much better off it you translate your passion into structure and systems that can be sustained in the long term and carried out by other ordinary people who are less motivated than you.

Commitment

For every potential business founder there is a moment of truth — "point of reality" — where the business concept has to be either brought into reality or given up.

At this point mental and financial commitments need to be made. This is the point at which the stage of business conception is completed and the stage of business setup starts.

The stronger the commitment, the more likely you are to succeed. If you move into the setup phase with thoughts of "let's see how we do," you are much more likely to fail than if you go into that phase with a one hundred percent conscious commitment and the attitude, "I'm going to make this work whatever obstacles are thrown in my way."

REAL-LIFE STORY

In 1996 I had the pleasure of meeting a young lady called Ellen MacArthur in a picturesque harbor in Dartmouth on the south coast of the United Kingdom. She was eighteen years old and was sailing her tiny twenty-one-foot yacht, Iduna, single-handedly around the United Kingdom

In 2001 Queen Elizabeth gave her an MBE (member of the Order of the British Empire), she was runner-up in the Sports Personality of the Year Awards, and she has is now the world's most famous yachtswoman, with a sponsorship package worth millions.

In 1996 she sent a letter to 5000 people looking for sponsorship to take part in a yacht race called the Mini-Transat, a single-handed transatlantic yacht race for the world's most innovative and radical twenty-one-foot yacht. She received just a few responses but none led to any significant support. Today, she is hot property.

At the time she lived and worked in an eight by six-foot cabin in a boat yard on the south coast of England. She existed on a budget of little more than one dollar per day for food. She worked all day on boats for very little money and worked all night on fulfilling her dream. After so much rejection and so little support, most people would have given up or, at the very least, had doubts about their chances. Not for one second did Ellen's enthusiasm or commitment dip. Failure was simply not an option. The race day was getting closer and closer, she had no boat and very little money. Her enthusiasm was infectious. There was a look of steely determination in her eyes and a self-confidence that never waned.

At the time I had entered into a joint venture with a FTSE-100 company. My suggestion of a very modest sponsorship was met with laughs of incredulity. What a mistake they made in hindsight. In the end Ellen's parents came to the rescue, but she was so committed that nothing would have stopped her taking part.

The moral of this story is that "where there is a will, there's a way," no matter how much the odds seem to be against you. If it were easy to set up your own business and make it successful, everyone would do it. If the fire in you is great enough — and you will know if it is — go for it.

Dreams become reality when you take the first small step and all the subsequent steps you need to get you to your destination. Better learn to walk before you try to run and do things properly the first time rather than rush and make mistakes.

Imagine your business is a fine, tall building. In setting up, you are building the foundation that lies beneath the ground that enables your business to reach to the sky. If your foundation is insufficient, your business and dreams may well tumble down.

CHAPTER 5:
Business Set Up

BUSINESS SET UP INTRODUCTION

Once a decision has been made to start a business there are a hundred
and one things to do. Before you can start, you need to set up. At this
point the founders are usually full of excitement, enthusiasm is at fever
pitch, and the desire to start setting up is immense. Friends and family
by this stage are probably noticing the glint in your eye, a smile on your
face and you are probably monopolizing the conversation. In fact, your
mind is totally consumed with your business. You find it hard to go to
sleep because you are thinking about it; your mind is racing with all the
things that you have to do. You feel liberated and free — life has never
been so good!

Unfortunately, there is no set manual you can follow. If only there was a
book entitled, *How to Set up the Perfect Business Guaranteed to Be One
Hundred Percent Totally Successful* that you could follow.

The reality is there are hundreds, if not thousands, of books and
publications written about how to set up businesses, but unfortunately,
none of them come with guarantees that if you follow their advice your
business will be an instant and unmitigated success.

The first problem is that the definition of success is down to personal
interpretation. One man's personal success could easily be another's total
failure. Given that being in business is a journey that never ends, where
if you feel you have arrived you probably have nowhere to go, all you
can realistically do is look forward as far as your current horizon and set
milestones/waypoints on your journey and create definitions of success
for each waypoint.

While none of us can see into the future, it does not stop us creating a vision for our own futures that we would like to see materialize, something to work towards. While some businesses succeed by chance and luck, for most of us success is a direct result of our considered choices and actions. The starting point of business setup is to create your business vision; this is a development of your business conception and the ideas and motivations that drove you to start your business in the first place.

> *"The only place where success comes before work is in the dictionary."* — Vidal Sassoon

CREATING A POWERFUL BUSINESS VISION

The starting point is the end point. Imagine what you want to achieve, what your business future will look like if you are successful. You can then put in place plans and actions to achieve it.

"Company vision" is now part of the vocabulary of most management consultants and business gurus who consider that if an organization does not have a vision, then it lacks a clear statement of intent. It is, therefore, commonplace for even small businesses to issue vision and mission statements. These are invariably announced by senior management who introduce them with much excitement to employees, who are expected to buy in to the message behind the vision. The reality is that a business vision often lacks substance and can be meaningless to the majority of staff. It is for this reason that the reception from employees can often be, at best, complete indifference.

A simple explanation of vision and mission might be as follows:

Vision: Where does the business want to go and what does it want to be?

Mission: What is the business going to do to get there and become what it wants to be?

A vision defines the big goals, creates clear unambiguous high-level objectives, and provides a framework from which to achieve them. It also attempts to define the intangibles that are frequently ignored yet are highly significant. Documenting and explaining a vision is just as important as formulating it in the first place. Complete understanding and buy-in by employees is essential for the vision to be realized.

Your employees need to know what business you are in and where you want to go, to stand any chance of getting there. Just as important you need to understand how you intend to travel there.

Vision elements

Your vision should include the following elements:

❏ Your reason for being in business

❏ What business you are in

❏ Your ambitions and what size you want to be over a given time frame

❏ A definition of your culture

❏ A definition of your values

❏ Your beliefs about your market and the business world

❏ Benchmarking against other organizations

❏ Position in market (Do you want to specialize in high- or low-end products, be seen as high-quality or cheap and cheerful? Do you want to be a market leader or niche player?)

❏ What markets you want to be in (local, national, or international; what countries, market segments, vertical markets)

❏ Your expected life cycle

❏ The things that are most important to you

❏ A clear definition of how you would like to be perceived by your customers, shareholders, investors, employees, suppliers, and the market in general

Having a clearly defined vision means you will know where you are going, what you have to achieve and how you are going to achieve it. It therefore provides the very foundations on which your business can be built. Strategy, policies, procedures, targets, measures, working practices, etc. should all reflect your vision. You and each and every employee must live by your vision and continually refer to it.

BLUE WATER VISIONING™ — SETTING YOUR CREATIVITY FREE

Blue Water Visioning™ is a term used to describe unrestricted freethinking. Despite freedom throughout much of the modern world real free thinking is constrained by society and the environment around us all. In a business context freethinking is very important to business survival and success, yet it is rarely considered a major issue.

Blue Water Visioning™ is likely to include:

- Idea generation
- Problem solving
- Thinking outside the box in a pioneering spirit
- Dreaming
- Imagining and inventing
- Creating something from nothing more than the ideas in your mind

LESSONS FROM HISTORY

History shows that the great free thinkers of the world were so ahead of their times that they were often ridiculed and sidelined as being foolish or mad. It is often years later that they become revered for the vision and insight they had.

To challenge convention, to think the unthinkable, to dare to dream, let alone stand up and admit to it, is rare. Society conditions us for continual advancement, but this is usually at a relatively modest pace. Small advances are often unnoticeable, rather like a child growing up — you don't see them looking different or bigger if you are with them every day. For grandparents who don't see them often, the changes can appear quite remarkable. In business, everyone expects gradual changes. It is the fundamental, major ones that excite true entrepreneurs.

The industrial revolution, air transport for all, the age of computers and personal computers, the Internet, e-mail and satellite communications, etc. have all revolutionized the world. The future is in all our destinies; we can make of it whatever we want. Where the next revolutions will come from we can only speculate or imagine and make happen.

OFTEN THE ONLY LIMITS ARE OUR IMAGINATION AND BELIEF

Great people are often those who believed when others doubted or did not believe. Originality and courage of conviction have been responsible for many of mankind's greatest achievements. As a general principle, the achievement receives the accolades, not the originality or courage of conviction that enabled it to happen. Behind almost every great achievement of mankind lie countless failures. Nothing was achieved without trying; indeed failure is often a milestone on the road to success. You have not failed until you have given up.

Equally the value of achievements can be unseen. James Dyson originally offered his new vacuum cleaner designs to the major manufacturers, but they weren't interested. Years later, I am sure they regretted their decisions as his company devastated their market. Great sportspersons who achieve, such as Steve Redgrave, are as impressive for the skill, commitment, dedication, and pure hard work that they put in for years to achieve the moment of glory. It is not always the best that wins; it is the ones with the greatest desire and perhaps the best support too.

Fear of failure or the unknown makes people not want to try. We live in risk-averse society. It takes courage and determination to take risks, to do things others have not even dreamed or think is impossible.

DON'T FOLLOW MY LEADER — BECOME THE LEADER

We are a world of followers; there are very few leaders. In business particularly we are like a convoy of ships in a row, doing similar things in similar ways. One often talks of best practice and benchmarking against other organizations. If you take any industry, it is remarkable how similar different companies often are, there is often little to tell them apart. Best practice is a notion invented by consultants.

I believe that however good you are at something, you can always be better. What is good today is not necessarily good tomorrow. We all crave for structure and understanding, yet we are living in this fluid and dynamic world where everything is constantly changing. Surely those who are continually adapting to this ever-changing world are those who will ultimately thrive and prosper.

HOW MANY COMPANIES GIVE THOUGHT TO CREATIVITY, IDEAS, AND VISION?
The truth is probably not that many. The day-to-day pressures and routine work provide such enormous challenges, that it is difficult to find time to actually look beyond the horizon, to imagine what could be, what will be and what has to be. To actively do this is to pioneer in the business sense, to cast off the shackles of convention, to go where others have never been, to make and shape the new world.

FEW PEOPLE HAVE THE APTITUDE TO CREATE INSPIRING VISIONS
The world consists of all types of different people with different aptitudes and skills. Creating inspiring visions, generating innovative ideas, etc. is not something you can go to college to learn. It is a skill you are born with — it is in your genes and make-up and is part of your personality. It is something you are, not something you can become.

WORDS OF WISDOM

If you don't have the aptitude for creating inspiring visions, seek the help of others who do.

CREATING INSPIRING BUSINESS VISIONS ISN'T SOMETHING YOU DO EVERY DAY

Knowledge of the field in which visionaries practice is important to enable them to put their creativity and imagination into context. For example, marketers and graphic designers can spend much of their time dreaming up new marketing and design ideas. They have that natural creativity that enables them to develop ideas and views of the future, generally in the context of their normal work activities. Their attributes and skills are well recognized and accepted, yet few companies have the foresight to see that the same energy and creativity applied to marketing and design should be applied to their whole business at a very broad, high level.

Big companies need to be leading their markets with creative thinking

Big successful companies have the most to lose. Smaller, more nimble competitors can easily respond to a changing market or bring innovation, which changes the very nature of the market or business. Big companies on the other hand should have the financial and organizational muscle to research, innovate, test, and advance with the objective of staying ahead and leading rather than following. It is both embarrassing and damaging for a large company to have to respond after the horse has bolted. The bigger you are, the greater the customer visibility and the more your weaknesses are likely to be exposed. Ironically, while large companies can suffer the greatest threats, they can they have the greatest opportunities. To ignore them can be commercial suicide. History supports large companies being usurped by small, determined challengers who ultimately become the giants themselves, and so the cycle continues.

The difference between strategy and visioning

High-level consulting groups and professional service organizations advise large corporations on significant strategy issues. These are frequently based on market analysis and serious academic-based consulting theory. Practitioners will typically be experienced graduates with MBAs from good universities. They will know their stuff and are likely to offer good advice and guidance. These companies are sometimes accused of adopting a formulaic approach to business issues that are replicated with different customers.

Blue Water Visioning™ goes beyond the consultants' strategy to dream up, invent, create, imagine, and think the impossible. It takes away the existing reference points, turning everything on its head if necessary, to see what may lie ahead. It is the articulation of instinct for spotting trends and future developments, often before others are remotely aware of them. It seeks out the possibilities within the external world.

Having shaped the possibilities of what might be, the strategy and professional service organizations can help verify and test the ideas, to map out ways that they can be implemented, and to fully analyze costs and benefits, and put the detail into a plan that can be executed.

HOW DO YOU IMPLEMENT BLUE WATER VISIONING™?

The best analogy for Blue Water Visioning™ is that of the creative advertising or marketing agency that takes a detailed brief from the clients and then comes up with a raft of ideas, themes, and suggestions. The client then gives feedback, the agency works on new ideas, and then makes new suggestions until such time as the client makes choices, initially relating to the broader aspects, but then to the detail until the project is finished.

Everyone, without exception, has ideas, and all ideas should be welcomed from anyone. Ideas for ideas' sake are not as valuable as ideas with direction and purpose. Some people are naturally gifted in business idea generation. This needs to be combined with knowledge of markets, businesses, and insight into future trends.

Blue Water Visioning™ is one of my great passions. For medium and large organizations, I have put together a program that involves rapid development of ideas. Normally it would involve senior management or project teams. The project takes place at an inspiring venue, perhaps a super yacht somewhere or a villa in a stunning location. It is important to be somewhere inspiring, away from the normal business environment. If you are interested in using this program email: **enquiry@asapinstitute.com**

LINKING IDEAS TO REALITY

Having an idea is one thing, but turning it into reality is something very different. It is easy to assume at an early stage that you will be able to set things up in a particular way, yet when you start to put the meat on the bone things can look very different. The more you get involved in your business setup, the more you will discover. You need to shape your setup in light of the realities you discover. You must make a conscious effort to remain realistic and objective.

To help you do this, make a list of assumptions and test the validity of these in the best way that you can. Consider doing market research, test marketing, and investigating true costs. Asking friends or professional advisors for a reality check is also worth considering.

ITERATIVE DEVELOPMENT

Sometimes getting started is one of the hardest things to do. It is better to make a start and then review and amend as required to get things right. While it is clearly better to measure twice and cut once, it is simply not possible in all circumstances.

Sometimes knowing the right thing to do is hard. It is easy to procrastinate. There comes a time when you simply need to make a decision to do something and then change it if required in light of experience or increased knowledge. Any good business will continually progress making improvements. Accept change as a positive necessity.

BUILDING IN FLEXIBILITY

If you recognize that change is a necessity, build flexibility into your plans and preparations. An example of this might be that you grow quicker than you originally anticipate. If you have bought an office or entered into a long lease, it can become very difficult and expensive to move into bigger and more suitable premises. It is much better to take short-term rentals possibly in serviced business centers that offer low-cost administrative services such as receptionists, typing, or photocopying services. Building in flexibility will enable you to remain as agile as possible, able to respond to changing circumstances.

LOW-LEVEL OBJECTIVES

The high-level objectives defined in your vision are important, but they can only be realized by creating a series of detailed tangible low-level objectives that can be easily measured.

Imagine you are overweight and want to lose a few pounds. Your vision might be to lose weight, an admirable high-level objective, but without some more quantification, the concept is so general that you are unlikely to achieve your expectations. If, however, you set some clear objectives, you know specifically what you are trying to achieve and will be able to measure whether you have achieved them. In this case your objectives might be:

1. Lose twenty-four pounds within three months.

2. Never lose less than one pound per week.

You might additionally realize that to lose this weight you will need to set the following more detailed objectives:

1. Eat no more than 1200 calories per day.

2. Stop eating chips.

3. Run five miles per day.

Creating low-level objectives enables you to split complex or unmanageable goals into small, easy-to-manage chunks.

BUSINESS PLAN

Having created a vision and defined clear objectives for the future, now you need to create a business plan that defines the practical steps you need to take to achieve them. The more comprehensive your business plans the better.

OH, VERY WELL, DAD
-MAKE MONEY FAST
— PLEASE

The three key elements of your business plan are as follows:

- Sales
- Operational
- Financial

The difficulty in setting up a business is that the devil is in the detail, but because it is very easy to get absorbed within the detail, you fail to see the big picture and ignore the basic reasons you started the business in the first place.

Imagine your business as a picture postcard of a landscape with the sun and the sea, the land, trees, animals, and people. You can see this picture clearly and the balance between the different features. Imagine now that you put some binoculars to your eyes. Initially you see the same picture; you then start to zoom in. The more you zoom in the less of the big picture you see and the narrower your field of view. You can see less but what you can see can be seen in great detail.

You need to be able to see all the different parts of the picture in great detail, but also you need to be able to see all the parts together. The big picture is comprised of lots of small parts, which all need to be in place or the big picture is spoiled. In nautical terms, if each part is a link in a chain, your business is only as good as its weakest link.

The purpose of the business plan is to enable you to work out what you need to do and by when, and what resources and skills you require to achieve the outcomes that you previously defined in your vision, as far ahead as your first way point. In effect, your starting point is your end point from which you plan backwards to the current time. Business plans are like the lightweight version of your business blueprint.

Hazards to avoid

One of the greatest mistakes business founders make in setting up a business is: first, not having a clearly defined vision of what they are trying to achieve; second, not having a business plan dovetailed to achieve the vision; and third, creating a business plan and then not following it. I suggest that many people create business plans to satisfy banks so that they can borrow money to establish their business and not for their own use in establishing the business. Creating a good business plan is difficult, but executing it is usually even more difficult.

Imagine what it would be like to be given the opportunity to drive a Formula One racing car in a race alongside Michael Schumacher. You might know how to drive your family car, but a Formula One car is the exact opposite. They both have four wheels, they both have an engine, and they both have a steering wheel of sorts, but there the similarity ends. First there are the racing rules — a world apart from the laws governing driving. Then there are the etiquette and the protocols, the team orders. The car is full of controls that you have little idea how to use, and then there is the power, which is simply terrifying. You put the car in gear, take your foot off the clutch and the car leaps forward uncontrollably. The shock disengages your brain and you have difficulty even steering and using the brakes. When you do find the brakes the wheels lock and you disappear forward into your straps yet more terrified. You finally make it around the circuit and begin to feel a little more in control. The race officially starts and other cars come whizzing past you at high speed. There is so much information on your car's computer that you simply cannot take it in. The team is talking to you on the radio, and you cannot concentrate on what they are saying. It is difficult enough getting around the next corner, let alone thinking of race tactics. Quite simply, you are hurtling out of control.

Setting up a new business can be a similar experience, with so much to think about, so much to do and apparently not enough time. You can easily become the victim of events and circumstances not the master of them. Meanwhile, experienced established business founders are cool, calm, collected, and firmly in control of their destinies. They may well be your competitors, totally committed to making sure that you do not succeed and that you do not steal their customers.

If you do not have lots of issues to deal with at this stage, there is a very good possibility you have not thought of everything and you are doomed to have lots of weak links that will limit your chances of success. It is not easy!

Developing your business model

Most business leaders do not fully understand the concept of a business model. One person who did was Ray Kroc, the man behind McDonald's. The concept is simple to grasp but rather more difficult to implement. The objective is to effectively create a winning business formula that is proven to work time and time again. This can be seen working in large successful corporations and franchise operations.

For the ten years I worked for the Mobil Oil Corporation, I was involved in retailing petrol in the United Kingdom. If you went to any Mobil gas station anywhere in the world you would instantly recognize it as a Mobil gas station. The big Mobil sign was an obvious give-away, as was the red Pegasus sign, which was a powerful global brand image. If you looked closer you would see similarities in many areas, from the round shapes on the canopies to the signage, pump types, and uniforms of the staff. For the inexperienced, it would be difficult to tell the difference between petrol stations owned and run by Mobil, owned by Mobil and run by tenants, and those independent petrol stations run by their owners. The advantages for all parties involved were numerous, including brand loyalty and recognition by customers and the leverage of considerable economies of scale by centralized purchasing of auto cleaning equipment, convenience products for sale in the stores, etc.

If you look at any successful business, you will see an operational model for generating shareholder value and for creating and delivering products and services to customers . The success of the model reflects the success of the business.

A business is like a machine with lots of components, each needing to fulfill its specific function to enable the whole machine to operate. If one likens a business to a ship, the various systems are easy to recognize. There is a propulsion system, which drives the ship. There is a fuel system, which provides fuel to the engines to enable the ship to be driven. There is a power system that provides electricity to run the other systems in the ship. There are electrical systems that deliver electricity to every part of the ship. There are navigation systems, steering systems, communication systems, emergency systems such as lifeboats and life rafts and fire fighting systems, damage control systems. Then there are the people-related systems, heating systems, lighting systems, shelter systems to provide accommodation for the crew, food production systems involving food storage, cooking, and serving systems. Huge numbers of systems operate together to enable the ship to function. A system is not just machinery or equipment; it is the sequence of processes and interactions that enable them to function. It is also human intervention for a sophisticated machine is useless if there is not a human being available to turn it on.

Elements comprising a system

Actions	Plans	Preferences	Interfaces
Processes	Strategies	Restrictions	Connection points
Events	Objectives	Limitations	Contacts
Commands	Policy	Attitude	Content
Controls	Audits	Motivation	Context
Measurements	Resources	Hierarchy	Conversions
Roles	Technology	Organization	Copies
Responsibilities	People	Relationship	Requests
Performance	Equipment	Preferences	Macros
Decisions	Facilities	Restrictions	Masters
Documents	Behavior	Limitations	Templates
Data	Attitude	Constraints	Critical path
Stored data	Motivation	Commands	Customization
Sequential data	Hierarchy	Instructions	Databases
Direct data	Organization	Comments	Knowledge bases
Activities	Relationship	Configurations	Defaults

Establishing your infrastructure

All businesses need an infrastructure to support them. The basics include the following:

- Name
- Legal establishment — corporation, limited partnership, sole proprietor
- Premises or address
- Bank account
- Phone number
- Fax number
- Stationery
- Web site
- E-mail account

Some businesses require significant infrastructure, others require virtually none. The objective should always be to find balance between the ideal infrastructure and costs you can afford to incur.

REAL-LIFE STORY

My wife, Jennifer, has worked with children all her life. She was brought up on a diary farm and can milk a herd of cows and drive a tractor. When she left school, she decided she wanted to work with children and qualified as a nursery nurse. From her remote rural upbringing, she moved to London to work as a live-in nanny.

Jenny has always put others first. She is caring and dedicated and has adored the children she has cared for, looking after them with love and dedication, as if they were her own. In her early career she agreed to stay with one family while the husband was ill, and in another, she agreed again to stay after handing in her notice when the parents went through a divorce. Such love and caring has its effects, and she still remains in touch with some of the children she looked after as babies and toddlers, who are now grown-ups.

In an amazing situation, two young British travelers met in New York and started discussing their childhood. One was talking about Jenny, the wonderful nanny she had when she was young.

The boy said he, too, had a fantastic nanny when he was young, named Jenny. Would you believe it, the nanny was one and the same person?

One family Jenny worked for sent their children to a Montessori nursery school. Jenny took a part-time job there along with her nanny position. It gave her real experience and confidence and made her think about her childhood dream of having her own nursery school. For a break and some thinking time, Jenny bought an around-the-world ticket and took a year off. She visited many countries and was also able to work in and visit nursery schools in Australia and America.

On returning to England, she took a flat, a daily nanny job, and enrolled in an evening course to qualify as a Montessori teacher. She would work a full day and then spend the evening studying.

For her, the Montessori Method of education was inspiring and she soon felt this was the type of nursery school she wanted to own. Once qualified, she worked as a Montessori teacher in a school in Buckinghamshire in the United Kingdom. She was soon promoted to head teacher, and she loved her work.

Within a year, she felt ready for the next step to own a school. By that time we had met. Together we searched for suitable premises until, through a good contact, we found a village hall in Oxfordshire. From finding the premises in February to the grand opening in August ready for a September start, it was not all smooth sailing. Some villagers felt it was a massive change to the use of the hall and the school would cause a traffic problem. Some quite hostile comments and gestures were directed at Jenny and the school.

Also Jenny continued teaching until July in what was then her current job. The owner experienced some problems that led to an abrupt closure of the school. With many unhappy parents and children, we rallied around and set up a temporary afternoon school that the children named "Blackberry School" in premises kindly offered by a stranger. In the morning Jenny took small groups of children into my house while I was at work in London. Looking back, it seems a remarkable story, considering childcare is heavily regulated and we had to gain relevant approvals in such a short time. Sometimes fate or unforeseen circumstances influence the creation of businesses.

Jenny is no entrepreneur, but she had a long-standing, burning desire to work for herself. I provided the entrepreneurial encouragement and support. She is not someone who can be pushed down a path she does not choose. Jenny welcomes advice, but she will always make her own decisions and reject advice if she doesn't like it.

As an owner running her own school, Jenny would have total control and freedom to do things just the way she wanted. This in itself was reason enough to forge ahead, but Jenny also had the support of many of the parents whose children's school had been closed.

Together we produced a business plan and strategy and applied for financial support from a government program. This involved attending business planning courses. Eventually Jenny was accepted into the program, which gave her a small income. The government program took a video of Jenny's business to use as an example to promote their scheme.

On the very important morning of the school's grand opening, the company manufacturing the furniture failed to deliver. I rushed off to a cheap furniture store to buy some self-assembly shelves. With just an hour to go to the opening, Jenny was busy trying to set up the school, while I built the shelves with her dad, Brian. Her mum, Betty, prepared traditional British cream teas with scones for the customers.

As the door opened and the first potential customers walked in, the finishing touches were just about complete. We were all exhausted but on a real high. There is a wonderful pioneering spirit in setting up any new business. You create a promise to your customers with a new business. You have no track record to rely on, which has both advantages and disadvantages.

After just two years she opened a second school, which also became successful. Jenny then had the vision of a Montessori Teachers' Club to share project ideas, classroom tips, etc. We set this up and had loyal members from all over the world. We also designed a range of Montessori furniture and equipment to sell to other schools. When our second baby, Xanthe, arrived, Jenny scaled back the growing business empire. She sold her second school for a handsome fee and closed down the furniture and equipment operations. As a business owner, you can choose to make your business fit your life.

What stands out is the massive amount of work that was involved in setting up the business and ensuring it remained successful. Behind any great success usually lies considerable hard work. For all that and frequent heartache, Jenny receives tremendous pleasure and fulfillment from her business. It has given her status and respect, not that she is interested in that. She has been able to maintain a business that upholds the highest standards and is greatly respected by the most discerning customers. She is changing lives, giving young children a firm foundation on which to base their futures. The four-year-olds she started with are now nearly adults. Jenny's business is not about money, it is about creating a worthwhile vision and being able to live her values without compromise.

Starting any new business takes courage and sacrifice to achieve success. For some people, success means money, but for others, like Jenny, it represents something different. You need to decide what success means to you.

Your business voyage may be full of surprises of every kind; there are things within your control and circumstances beyond them. Accept with courage the challenges you face, be magnanimous with your success, and resilient with your failures. Remember that business is a journey, and if you think you have arrived, you have probably nowhere to go.

Chapter 6:
The Business Voyage

THE BUSINESS VOYAGE INTRODUCTION

The business setup stage finishes and the business voyage commences at the point at which you start trying to trade. In other words the point at which you contact potential customers with a product or service to offer and the ability to deliver should you be successful in securing an order.

Using a nautical analogy, the setup phase is the design and construction of your ship, the ship being the business. The transition phase is the launch and commissioning of your ship, the voyage commences when the commissioning is complete, the crew is assembled and you set to sea on your voyage. As the business owner it is your ship, you chose it, you designed it, and you had it built with a specific purpose and intention in mind. As we discussed earlier, businesses exist to meet the needs of their owners, which is delivering shareholder value that, in real terms, is likely to mean creating profit and/or equity value. You decided whether you wanted a cruise liner, an oil super tanker, a very large container ship, a tug, or a racing yacht. You decided whether it was big or small, whether it had giant global aspirations or small local aspirations. You set up the systems, you chose the crew, you set the course, and you stand accountable. You may or may not have defined the working life of your ship, in other words, how long you expect your business to last. Do you expect it to be around in two months, two years, twenty years, or two hundred years? Are you planning to sell to somebody else? Or perhaps acquire other ships to form a fleet? Are you emotionally attached to your ship? Or is it just a means to an end?

First timers face the prospect of being the captain of their own ship. Only time will tell whether you will sink or float.

This chapter explores different aspects of a business life, with a view to understanding some of the issues, which influence business success, but are not commonly discussed in traditional business education.

OVERCOMING INERTIA

Nothing happens unless you make it happen. Sometimes you can have all the components of your business in place, yet the business itself doesn't want to start moving. Getting your first customers may be the most difficult. Without customers you are simply dead in the water going nowhere. Any effective business should be a series of chain reactions. This might be a customer placing an order resulting in a purchase order being made against suppliers resulting in raw materials for a factory to turn into new products, which results in deliveries, invoices, and, ultimately, cash going into the bank account.

An analogy might be a young child trying to make a snowball roll down a steep hill. The child scoops a handful of snow and shapes it into a ball. She puts it on the ground and it sits there doing nothing. The eager child encourages the snowball along, pushing it with her hands. Initially there is lots of resistance but as the child continues to roll the snowball, it starts to collect new snow becoming bigger and bigger. As the weight increases and the hill gets steeper, the snowball starts to roll easier and easier becoming faster and faster until it needs no pushing at all to go rolling down the hill.

Work out what it is that could hold your business back and come up with a strategy to address these issues. I recommend you make a list of all the things you could possibly think of and address each one. In doing this you are removing all excuses for failure and, therefore, setting yourself up for success.

DIFFERENT WAYS TO ACHIEVE THE SAME RESULTS

There can be many ways to achieve the same result. It is very important to achieve results in the most efficient manner. In most situations it is easy to be drawn in by convention and preconceived beliefs that we all hold. Invariably, if you try to look at anything objectively it is possible to see ways things could be done better and more efficiently. Reducing the cost of sales will increase profits.

Do not let a day go by without thinking about how you can increase your profitability. Never become complacent, no matter how well you're doing.

NASTY EXPERIENCES

The business world can be a very tough one. All business owners will sooner or later find themselves faced with very unpleasant situations to deal with. These may include disputes with employees, customers, suppliers, or even regulatory authorities. To any decent person these disputes can become very unpleasant indeed. They can become emotionally distressing and can cause a significant amount of stress. I have noticed, people who are new to business can be severely shocked. It can be difficult to believe if you are a decent and honest person to find that others can attack you, verbally and financially, when you are innocent. Some people will use bullying as a deliberate tactic to get their way. People will argue that black is white and vice versa and they will make you question your own judgment. It is easy to begin to think they might be right and you might be wrong. While this obviously may be the case, in many situations your assessment will be completely right.

The problem with any dispute is that it is likely to persist and fester unless you resolve it one way or another. This can be very difficult. Reason and the truth are no benefit when dealing with somebody who appears to be unreasonable and a liar. I am sure psychologists may be able to come up with explanations, but as a business owner, you have to respond to the realities of each situation as you find it. I advise you to not respond in emotional ways to the people with whom you are in dispute. Remain polite and respectful at all times, even if subjected to abuse yourself. Continually refer to the facts and make your position as clear as possible. Try to make an assessment of the effects of the dispute on your business and you personally. Make an assessment of exactly what your opponent would like to achieve and think very carefully about the options open to you. Even if your opponent is completely wrong, it may be in your best interest to give him what he wants to settle the dispute. Taking somebody to court can be costly in terms of legal fees and your time. If you win, there is no guarantee the person will comply with the court orders. There is also no guarantee that justice will prevail. The bad guys often win and the reality is that the world is full of injustice.

In the United Kingdom employees can take their employer to an industrial tribunal if they feel they have been wrongfully dismissed or if they believe an employer is in breach of their contract of employment. An employer is forced to defend their employees' claims in a court of law however preposterous the employees' claims may be. An employer can lose on the smallest procedural technicality.

In the course of my business career, I have had the misfortune of having to attend a number of these industrial tribunals on behalf of employers. One case that was lost related to one of the worst employees anyone could have had the misfortune to have employed, a person who was discovered to have attempted to divert contracts worth hundreds of thousands of dollars away from the business to him personally. It was an absolute travesty of justice that he won his case. He won because the company modified his duties in light of their discoveries about his alleged improper conduct while investigations were ongoing, which was specifically permitted in his contract of employment. The judge ruled that despite this being contractually permitted he felt it was unfair given the fact that the employee was not consulted. Sometimes the law is an ass. There is nothing more galling than to experience the gloating of the bad guy having won.

I have heard many stories from business owners in every field imaginable having to deal with the most unpleasant situations. As a business the laws often seem stacked against you. When you start up in business you cannot imagine that you are going to become the victim, but if you are in business long enough I promise you, your turn will come.

THE POWER OF WORDS

Words can bring happiness or sadness, success or failure, wealth or poverty. What you say and what you write will determine the outcomes you receive. It is strange that few people recognize the true power of words. Learn to use words well and you will flourish.

In 1998 I wrote my first book, which became an international best seller, ran to three editions, and was sold throughout the world with reprints in different languages including Korean. As a result of this, I received inquiries from hundreds of companies throughout the world. I was able to influence opinions of some of the highest paid business and technology consultants in the world. The book enabled me to enter into a joint venture in the range of $750,000 with one of the United Kingdom's top one hundred businesses and, subsequently, helped me raise approximately $7.5 million through an IPO of my business which resulted in a personal equity worth in excess of $40 million. The words in my company's prospectus persuaded 1000 people to invest in my business.

Words deliver your promise to your customers, words define the contractual terms of contracts, and words persuade customers to buy from you and suppliers to supply you. Never underestimate the power of words. Learn to use them to your advantage, and treat them with respect.

One highly successful U.K. entrepreneur, Gerald Ratner, grew a successful chain of jewelry stores that were located throughout the United Kingdom. The business was listed on the London Stock Exchange and had a very large valuation. One day the overconfident Gerald Ratner was doing a presentation to 6000 business people when he made the off-the-cuff comment that the sherry decanter his firm sold was "crap." When he said this he was trying to be funny. What happened next was probably one of the quickest failures of a successful business in U.K. corporate history. The journalists reported his comments which resulted in a collapse in both shareholder and customer confidence that lead to the failure of the business.

"Within months of that fateful comment in April 1999, Ratner was a broke, unemployed laughing-stock. Five hundred million pounds had been wiped off the value of the Ratner chain, the family firm he had built into a multi-million-pound empire. He lost a £6 million fortune, his £600,000-a-year job, and his name, once emblazoned across hundreds of High Street stores, was humiliatingly junked." (Source: *The Sunday Times* — "U.K. Business Week")

LEVELS OF AWARENESS

The world is full of mystery. The more you search for understanding the more you will learn, but you will also discover how much more there is to learn. With understanding comes knowledge and with knowledge comes power — power to make informed choices and power to influences outcomes.

MATCHING EXPECTATIONS WITH REALITY

When you decide to conceive your business and set it up, you do so with some of the expectations of what results you expect to achieve. Nobody does things for no reason and with no understanding of the consequences of their actions. At regular intervals you need to assess how your expectations compare with the realities at that time. None of us can see into the future. We, therefore, have to make assumptions based on our past experience, our knowledge of what others have achieved in similar circumstances, and the advice of others. It's very important to define your assumptions during the planning and set up phases and also as you progress through the life of your business. Are you over- or under-achieving? Are your sales or profits higher or lower than you expected? Is it costing your more or less to deliver your products or services than you expected?

So much about the business world is intangible but the reality is fact. In other words, if you have made a profit, you have made a profit; if you have suffered a loss, you have suffered a loss. You have either won sales or not. Business success relies on making quality assessments based on what you know and what you think will happen.

Business is all about anticipating the future. This could be market demand, future pricing, manufacturing capability, or economic conditions. You can anticipate that interest rates might go down, but they might go up. A crystal ball or a time machine would be useful. If anyone creates one, please let me know!

THE BUSINESS HORIZON

Given that a major part of business life is anticipating the future, the extent to which you are able to meaningfully consider your business future is the point at which you can realistically look ahead. I call this point your "business horizon." Depending on how visionary and forward-thinking you are and the circumstances affecting the business you are in, the horizon period might be anything from a few hours or days to potentially many years. If you are a commodity trader in a highly volatile market, your horizon is going to be very close. If you run a convenience store in a small village where there is virtually no chance of a supermarket or indeed any competitor setting up in competition, then perhaps your horizon can be longer. There will always be the unexpected, the uncharted rock, the unpredicted storm or the rogue wave. Perhaps Target or Wal-Mart will introduce a low-cost, door-to-door delivery service, or an entrepreneurial local will establish a high-quality, exceptional-value mobile store that delivers twenty-four hours a day. Nothing in business is certain.

 It's important to be aware of what is over the horizon. Do everything in your power to find out. Buy a big telescope, climb up a big hill so you can see farther, send an advance party to see what they can see, use all the intelligence sources you can find, read articles, watch your competitors, and be prepared. Quite often the signs are there, the writing's on the wall. All you have to do is to take the time and the trouble to look.

By scrupulously paying attention to what's over the horizon, you can be prepared, amend your assumptions, create new plans, and set a new course whenever necessary.

SET YOUR COURSE

As a business leader you have the right to set your own course. You are the captain. You are in command, where you go and how you get there is up to you. In a business context this might mean entering new markets, launching new products, targeting new customers, or implementing new

strategies. You can't guarantee the outcomes, but you do get to make the choices and take the actions and you have to accept the consequences good and bad.

Business is a journey that never ends. During the journey, you will set many courses. Realistically you can only set courses to your points on your business horizon, which I call "waypoints." If your waypoints are useful and take you to where you want to go, use them again and keep using them while they continue to serve you. If they are not, set new waypoints. The more experienced you are, the better the course you are likely to set. There will always be high-risk courses and low-risk courses that offer high rewards and low rewards. You have to decide whether to take high- low, or medium-risk courses. A high-risk course might take you through a narrow, rock-strewn channel or an iceberg zone, but save you a huge amount of distance that, in turn, delivers a high return. The risk is that you will hit the rocks or the iceberg and sink completely or, at the very least, be seriously delayed while you embark upon a disaster recovery operation.

Steering a good course

Having set your course you need to be able to steer it. Anyone attempting to steer a ship for the first time will find it very difficult. The Ships wheel operates the ships rudder, which creates turning forces. If you are on course and the wheel is central, the wind and the waves, the rotation of the propellers and differences in the hydrodynamic flows over the hull will cause the ship to drift off course. The helmsman doing the steering therefore needs to bring the ship back on course.

Novices will turn the wheel to bring the ship back on course. The immediate effect is nothing, so they turn the wheel yet further. Slowly the ship starts to turn and the turn gets faster and faster. The ship passes the chosen course and keeps turning away from it. The helmsman panics, puts the opposite wheel on, nothing happens initially so he puts on more wheel, the ship then starts to turn in the opposite direction and the same thing happens going the other way.

If you were to look down on the ship from a helicopter you would see from its wake that it was moving like a snake. This uses lots of energy, is uncomfortable for the passengers and the journey takes considerably longer. By the same token, overcompensation in business can be disastrous. Be prepared to fine-tune.

In business sticking to your course is an important issue. There are many issues and people who may attempt to knock you off course, not the least of which is your competitors. Vigilance, keeping your eye on the ball, is key. Watch for trends and take action quickly to seize opportunities and defend against threats. Sticking to your course is about making choices and being committed to taking the actions necessary to see them through to fruition.

WORDS OF WISDOM
Distractions can be the death of a business.

Look for turning points and alter your course

If you are the captain of a fishing boat searching for fish, you set course for your chosen fishing grounds and start fishing. Having made your choice you need to start fishing to see what you will catch. After a while you have to assess how well you have done. If you give up immediately you will have wasted your journey and you might miss out on the fish that are just in front of you. If however, you have fished for days and caught nothing, you are probably right in thinking that the fish are elsewhere. This is the turning point, the point at which it is right and proper to alter course for new fishing grounds. Leaving too soon or doing it too late can be very costly.

In business, you make your plans and cast your net. If it doesn't work and you can't find customers, take stock, consider some alternatives, and set a new course.

Watch out for drifting off course

A ship steering a steady course can still drift off course and arrive at an unexpected destination by the effects of wind and tide and compass error. A business, too, can drift off course. At sea, the seascape can all look the same, so it is difficult to realize that you are off course without navigating properly and fixing your position.

Drifting off course assumes you are traveling forward or progressing, but all too often in business it is easy not be moving purposefully anywhere. When you do nothing, time moves on and your business will drift to wherever circumstances take it.

In a ship if you don't have the engine running or the sails set and you don't steer a purposeful course, you will drift around the oceans with the prevailing winds and currents, until you eventually run into hazards like rocks, when your voyage will inevitably end in tears.

I have been advising a newly established company that two friends run. While the business is running, they don't have enough revenue to satisfy their basic living requirements. As a result, they are working harder, putting in longer hours, and doing most jobs themselves to save money.

Two months ago, we discussed that they needed to address the root cause of their problem, which is not enough sales revenue. Their choices are simple, get new customers or do more business with existing ones or a combination of both. To achieve any of the options they need to put some effort into sales and marketing. They know what they need to do, but every week we have the same conversation where they repeat, "We must do something about it." They are drifting until they take action.

They are losing time; each day of no sales and marketing inactivity is one day further away from earning what they need to survive. They have high overheads with expensive premises, which need to be fully utilized. They are drifting because they are busy, tired, and too close to the day-to-day activities to realize what is happening. They are both highly intelligent people, but they, like the rest of us, have the capability to be overwhelmed with workload.

From time to time you need to fix your position in business, assess where you are compared with where you may think you are. Take action once you have established this. Have you achieved your sales and profit objectives? Is your cash flow situation under control? Have you been successful moving into new markets or opening up new accounts?

In summary, drifting is all about having terms of reference. Sailing across an ocean, the sea looks the same, yet when sailing close to land you can see when you are going nowhere. In business you need to be able to establish reference points to be able to measure progress. These may be setting sales or financial targets and measuring progress against them. If you don't have a destination, you are unlikely to end up where you want to be.

How would you know if you have drifted off course?

You will only know if you have a documented course in the first place which might be any number of different objectives defined in your business plans. Even if you have documented your course, you need to be able to measure and analyze to compare actual with planned.

How to keep on course

Measure often and take corrective actions often. There is no point in getting to the end of the year before you realize that you have not been achieving your objectives. By then it is too late to take corrective action. Measure daily, weekly, and monthly, and make small corrections along the way.

What to do when you get completely lost

Whatever anyone might say, there are times when all business leaders and ships' navigators will get completely lost. We hope this is short-lived. If it isn't, the best thing we can do is to seek outside assistance as soon as possible.

In business terms this might mean contacting and working with:

- Work colleagues
- Consultants
- Professional advisers
- Bank managers
- Business advisors

If you have lost your way, you are in the greatest danger and must treat the situation as a "mayday" emergency.

Don't be conned by success

Luck has its place in business. Sometimes it's possible to be at the right place at the right time with the right products or services. Being a tree surgeon immediately following a hurricane, selling generators during prolonged power failures, vaccine during an epidemic, boats during floods, or owning the last shrimp boat in the fleet after a great storm, as in *Forrest Gump*, is wonderful. In most cases we make our own luck by "laboring under correct knowledge." Many businesses are highly successful without knowing why.

"*One of the hardest things is to get the maximum out of a rising business. The worst sins are committed in boom times, when everyone feels satisfied. That's when managers get fat and arrogant.*" — Jack Welsh, ex-CEO of General Electric

WORDS OF WISDOM
Business can be more likened to a marathon than a sprint; it is all about pacing yourself.

Be prepared for all conditions
Your business, like a ship, will need to operate in all conditions. It is easy to be lulled into a false sense of security as you happily sail through calm and tranquil waters. It is just a matter of time before you have to face a storm. Everyone who remains in business will at some time have to battle adverse conditions. In business this might mean market slumps, economic downturns, attacks by competitors or staff defections.

Experienced mariners have great respect for their environment and so, too, do wise business leaders. When conditions deteriorate, you need to defend against the threats you face and protect yourself. If conditions become dire, you might be fighting for your survival.

When conditions are good, seize the opportunities and take advantage of them. These opportunities might be increased sales and profits growth, expansion and development.

Set your speed

Slow ahead; half ahead or full speed ahead, the choice is yours. Match your speed to your objectives and to the prevailing conditions. In buoyant market conditions, you can go for growth, but in recessions or difficult times you need to slow down.

Going too fast can have catastrophic consequences. You can wreck your ship (business) by overtrading and running out of cash and you might find that your infrastructure is not up to the strains, which might be placed upon it.

Comparing yourself with others by benchmarking can be a useful guide.

Know when you are not under command

When a ship is crippled in the water by engine or steering failure for example, it is classed as "not under command." The captain and crew are unable to proceed on their way or avoid dangers or other ships. They are helpless while the situation continues.

Businesses can of course come to a grinding halt when manufacturing machines fail; power outages prevent computers from working, or strikes mean there are no employees at work. These are events that are largely outside your control. However many businesses suffer from being "not under command," when their leaders abdicate their responsibility and simply stop giving directions to the business.

Don't stay anchored in the past

If business can be likened to a journey that never ends, being anchored means you are not moving and if you are not moving, it won't be long before you will be out of business.

No sales, no product or service development, no improvement initiatives are all signs that you might be anchored. Anchoring is something you do at the end of a voyage — the business end — not something you do along the way, for anything other than a very short time at least. Always look to the future while savoring the present; never live in the past.

CHANGE MUST BECOME A WAY OF LIFE

Change is something that most people find hard to deal with even if they deny it. Everyone has different thresholds of change tolerance. A small change for one person might be worrying, stressful, or irritating, while others might take it in stride. Understanding yourself and others will help you deal with the consequences.

With progress comes change. The challenge is to be in control of it rather than letting it be in control of you. As a business leader embrace change and make it a way of life rather than an unpleasant event.

USE CHANGE TO DELIVER CONTINUAL IMPROVEMENT

Each day you should look to improve your business and your private life. Small improvements may not seem like much on their own, but when you add them all up, they comprise a significant change.

The drive should be to continually question what you do and explore ways of improving. Sometimes the only way to find out for sure is to try. If it doesn't work, you have at least learned that.

NOTHING SHOULD EVER BE GOOD ENOUGH

Good enough is mediocrity. Strive for excellence in everything you do. There are constraints in any situation. A very large container ship  will never be as agile as a nimble warship. The point is to be the best you can be within the constraints you have. Many of the world's greatest achievements have been made with minimal resources, but purpose, commitment, effort, enthusiasm, courage, and determination will give you far more than you can imagine.

INTRODUCE A FEW ABSURDITIES

Military organizations are renowned for absurdities. Huge importance is given to what others may see as trivial things. Punishments can sometimes be seen as disproportionate to the offenses committed. To the outsider, they may seem bloody-minded or stupid, but over the years I have learned there is often method in the madness.

A few absurdities remind people that they are at work and are not free to do just as they wish. Business is a serious matter; it earns the money to pay for our subsistence and lifestyles.

One business leader I knew would never see staff members who were late for a meeting with him. They soon realized that he took their punctuality seriously and they were usually never late again. It all comes down to purpose and discipline.

If you are going to create an absurdity in your business, I suggest you think of something that will seriously impress your customers, exceed their expectations by going the extra mile. In one business, I have heard the telephone is never allowed to ring more than twice, in others every customer is greeted personally. A few absurdities can get you noticed, perhaps create amazing public relations, and will certainly set you apart from your competitors.

HOWEVER GOOD YOU ARE, YOU CAN ALWAYS BE BETTER

There is no business on earth that couldn't do better. Look to make improvements in everything, no matter how small the improvements may be. Small improvements on their own can be barely distinguishable, but add them together and they can comprise a significant trend.

The bigger and more successful your company is the more you have to lose, the smaller and less successful you are, the more you have to gain.

Small things do matter

Being better than your competitors or being good enough for your business to survive and thrive is normally a combination of many different small things. Each of these small things on their own may seem virtually insignificant but when added together, they make the difference.

To help you understand the small things that make a difference in your business, imagine yourself rising above your business in a helicopter. The higher you rise, the more you can see of your business, your competitors, your customers, and your market. What you are doing is taking yourself out of your business and trying to look at it from an outsider's point of view. When you are inside your business you can become blind to how others see you, you can become too close and too involved.

Take a pen and some paper and make notes about everything that is happening, what others are doing, in particular, customers. Imagine you are a potential customer of your business. What do you have to offer, how does that compare with your competitors, does your offering meet the needs of your potential customers? Be honest with yourself. What could you do to set yourself apart from your competitors? What could you do to impress customers and make them buy from you and, what things must you avoid doing? When you have finished the exercise, ask your friends and colleagues to give you some feedback and ask for their input. Better still, ask your customers. Categorize all your points and come up with an action plan.

Many years ago I was involved in Petrol Retailing, running eighteen of Mobil Oil Company's highest-volume petrol stations in Northwest London and surrounding regions. Petrol retailing is a tough business that operates 24/7, three hundred sixty-five days a year. Motorists are tough customers. Let's face it, we don't derive pleasure from buying fuel for our cars. Competition is intense and in the majority of instances highly price-sensitive. Much as oil companies try to differentiate their fuel, to most customers, fuel is fuel wherever you buy it. An oil company can invest millions to build a lovely new gas station, but to make it successful you have to do more than just open your doors. Signage is highly important, as is the appearance and lighting. Ease of access on and off the site can be a make or break factor. No motorist wants to stop at a gas station where the traffic is running so fast they have to wait for ages to get back onto the main road. No one wants to pick up a dirty fuel nozzle or stand in a pool of spilled fuel, cleanliness is therefore important. How frustrating it is to pull up to a pump put your nozzle in the car and find out the pump is out of order. Equally imagine the rage you would feel to find out the pump had only dispensed a small fraction of what you had been charged for. You would not be too pleased either, if you were out for the night or on the way to an important business meeting and the pump had not stopped and sprayed you with gas.

Nobody enjoys waiting in line to pay, particularly when you are in a hurry. You want to be in and out of the store as quickly as possible. The lighting must work at night and customers must feel safe and secure. Customers expect that you will have a toilet; they will feel disgusted if it is dirty or there is no paper. They might also expect to be able to check their tire pressure, or be able to wash their windshield. They might want to empty their ashtray or litter into a can, so it would be helpful if you had one and ensured there was enough room in it to take their rubbish.

These points are the absolute basic requirements you would need to stand any chance of succeeding. You are not going to sell anything in your gas station store if you do not have any stock. Equally you are unlikely to sell much if your shelves are stocked with row upon row of undesired or useless objects. You have to sell what people want and need. Clean bright shops, well organized into clearly marked sections, with full, clean shelves with merchandise moved to the front, labels facing the forward, will sell. Location is important; the counter has a hot spot near the checkout, where the right fast-moving items can sell like hot cakes. The appearance and attitude of the staff is also vitally important.

I could go on an on, but I feel this illustrates graphically the point of how small things matter. Whatever your business involves, work out what small things matter to your customers, then do something about it.

Set rules and controls before the event, not after

If a ship sets to sea and enters a storm, it is a little late to tie down the best dishes and glassware, as it will already be in pieces all over the deck. The same is true in business. You can't turn the clock back, much as it would be good if you could.

If something can go wrong in business, it often will. As a new business leader, it is easy to think the best of people, but remember, to others your business might be just a job, they might not care if you win or lose. They certainly are unlikely to have your commitment and dedication or indeed understanding; if they did, they would have your job. It is easy to think, "It won't happen to me," until it does. Quite often, those who you think are your best people will let you down the most.

On a positive note, rules and controls help people understand what you expect of them. How can you blame them for something happening if you didn't give them proper guidance?

If you have been in business for any time, you are likely to have had some first-hand experiences. The effort of setting proper rules and giving clear guidance will save a lot of time and probably expense later on. There are so many legal requirements and regulations in business that the penalties for not setting rules and giving guidance can lead to criminal prosecution and even imprisonment, particularly relating to health and safety issues.

Know when to ask for assistance

On your voyage there will be times when you need to stop and ask for directions, times when you return to port for a refit, times when to seek the professional services of others such as surveyors, harbor pilots, specialist engineers, etc. If things go horribly wrong, you need to send out an SOS and ask for emergency assistance, or face the consequences of sinking without a trace.

Business is just the same; you need advice and help from time to time. Some is free and some will cost you. Failing to take advice, taking it too late, or worse still, receiving bad advice can be disastrous.

AVOIDING DISASTER

If you consider all the world's disasters, a large number of them could have been predicted. Build a town under an active volcano, or a city on the edge of a tectonic plate, or a port in an area known for tsunamis, and to those with any common sense, there is a disaster waiting to happen. Send a ship to sea with an incompetent and untrained crew or without any means of navigation and it's hardly surprising that a disaster is highly likely to follow. Even storms can be forecast.

Looking for signs

There are usually some signs that precede a disaster; you just have to be aware of what to look for, then keep an eye out for them. In the case of a ship at sea, it can be a weather forecast, a seismograph, or minor earth tremors.

In the business context read the papers, look for trends in sales, customers starting to cancel orders, politicians discussing policies, world crises brewing. Very rarely are there no signs at all. Even history has its place in giving insights into what might happen in the future.

Taking action to avoid obstacles

Once you have seen the signs, you must take action. If your ship is a Titanic and you see the iceberg coming, alter course, take avoiding action, close your watertight doors, and make preparations. If you see a storm coming, batten down the hatches, alter your course and go around it. Stay in port or, if you are determined to set sail and weather the storm, be prepared.

If you see a price war looming with your competitors, decide whether you can afford to fight it. Is the risk worth the effort? Is war inevitable? Is there any way you can avoid it? You can't change your past, but you can change your future. As a business leader, you have the ability to make choices and to take actions. The quality of these choices and actions will determine to a great extent the outcomes you experience.

Gripping difficult situations

The more difficult a situation is, the greater the hesitation of a business leader to grip it and take positive action. Natural instinct is to shy away from difficult things. It is easier to leave them, ignore them, or just as bad, deliberately not look for fear of finding something we don't want to find. "Out of sight, out of mind," is a relevant saying. All businesses have difficult situations from time to time, problems with staff, customers, or suppliers.

When you discover situations and don't deal with them, they fester and get worse. Dealing with them is one of the more undesirable aspects of leading a business, but that is your job as much as doing the things you enjoy.

In the long run you will feel so much better when you have dealt with the difficult issues. Festering, difficult situations will cause you stress and anxiety and will damage the business.

Try and detach yourself personally and apply your values to the situation. It is you in the role of business leader taking the actions and making the decisions, not you in the role of your private life.

DISASTER RECOVERY

What would happen if your ship hit the rocks? Do you have policies and procedures in place, which would enable your crew to save the ship? If the engines failed, is there a back up? If your ship springs a leak, do you have the equipment and skills to stem it? What would you do if your crew mutinied? What would you do if you lost your way? Whose advice would you seek to get back on course?

Business is risky, full of ups and downs, twists and turns and unexpected events. You don't have to be a rocket scientist to anticipate the dangers we have previously identified. As they say in the Royal Navy, "prior planning prevents poor performance." This is the "5p" rule, i.e., a little bit of investment up front can save a huge expense later on.

OVERCOMING ADVERSITY

I like reading autobiographies of successful entrepreneurs. Almost without exception they have overcome adversity on more than one occasion. Adversity in many cases is near ruin and destruction, not simply a few things going wrong. I have experienced it myself on so many occasions I am never surprised.

When things do go wrong in your business, it causes immense personal stress. When things do go wrong as they undoubtedly will, you can go into shock, which clouds your thinking and prevents you from taking the positive actions necessary to deal with the situation. Remain calm and collected and think through your alternatives carefully. Whatever you do, don't become a headless chicken. Be careful not to act in haste or you might find yourself regretting it for a long time.

I love sailing, particularly ocean sailing. When you set sail across a mighty ocean in a small yacht, you abandon the safety net of civilized society and rely on your own resources. When the engine or generator breaks down, you can't call in the repairman. When your yacht is on fire, you can't call the fire brigade. If you run out of necessities, you can't just run down to the convenience store. When there is a stiff breeze from behind, fast sailing, a rolling blue ocean with bright sunshine, life is good, your senses are heightened. But when it is bad, you are in a storm that goes on for days and days, the waves are breaking and rolling over the boat, you are tired, wet, and hungry. It is awful. Business can be the same.

When times get tough, your crew, like fairweather friends, may well get off and leave you, abandon what they consider to be a sinking ship. Your bank manager may be charming during the good times, eager to lend you money you don't need, pleased to call you his partner, yet when times are tough and you need him most, he may well be the complete opposite and not be there for you. You won't be the first and you won't be the last to suffer from supposed friends turning against you. Suppliers too may withdraw their credit and customers may attempt not to pay you in the hope that you might go bust and they'll never have to pay.

Never rely too heavily on anyone, never believe everything people tell you, and look out for knives aimed at your back. The business world has hard edges. Other people, even those you trust the most, may lie, cheat, and steal. Even when you have the law on your side, don't expect justice one hundred percent of the time.

MANAGING PAPERWORK AND CLUTTER BUSTING

When you are busy it is easy to sink under a mountain of paper and clutter. Creating a business means you create an opportunity for other businesses that see you as their potential customer. The bigger, more successful and higher profile you are the more people will be contacting you via mail, e-mail, fax, and telephone. Often what starts as a trickle can turn into a flood of huge proportion. Your mailbox may well seem to fill up again almost as soon as you have emptied it. Your fax machine may start to wear out, burdened with its daily incoming messages. Not only can this use lots of expensive paper and toner, but faxes you want to receive from customers with orders can get lost in a sea of junk faxes. E-mail spam is irritating enough. These days it is possible to have anti-spam filters and delete large numbers of e-mails with a couple mouse clicks. Headers and the sender's details simplify spam identification.

Mail received through the postal service, however, can all look the same, and it is often difficult to know what is important and what is junk. Paper can become your enemy, swamping your desk and your office. Not only does it do this, it affects your mind, your efficiency and your state of wellbeing, it can cost you money too. What is more, you may not be able to stop it arriving even if you want to. In some countries there are registers you can join that are used by direct mail marketers and fax broadcasters to stop sending correspondence people don't want to receive. Even if you register on these, you are still likely to receive some junk mail.

It can seem laughable to see a rising mountain of mail and paperwork as a very serious business issue, but it is. It traps you like a fog preventing you from seeing what is important and disorienting you. Do you have an in tray? How often to do you sort it out? Is it cleared every morning or does it tend to get bigger? Do you have piles of paper on your desk or is your desk cleared every day? In an ideal world you need to deal with your paperwork on a daily basis, throwing away junk or paperwork once it has served its purpose, acting upon things that need action, and filing everything else so that you can find it when you need it. I am continually amazed at how much time can be wasted looking for things in overflowing in trays and piles of papers.

Most businesses need to sort out clutter and paperwork regularly. Throw away or sell off unwanted things, create structured storage, and create systems. Archive old items that you need to keep like accounting records and put them into storage.

Not all unsolicited mail is junk. You can educate yourself, find new suppliers, hear about special offers that can save you money, and find ways of improving your business. You can also learn how the professionals get results. What catches your attention and why. You may need to send unsolicited mail or faxes to attract new customers.

DRESS FOR SUCCESS

What you wear affects how you feel about yourself and how others perceive you. It reflects your character, your values, and your standards. It is true that first impressions count when meeting new clients or suppliers. How much employees respect you may depend on your personal appearance.

Different businesses may determine different clothing. An auto mechanic would look foolish in a suit. Creative business people might be expected to wear casual clothing where the corporate world would definitely expect to see suits or smart formal business dress.

I recall grasping the power of clothing when I joined the Royal Navy. The range of uniforms was enormous and was based upon the activity, the location, and the time of day. I find it amazing how looking smart can lift your spirits, increase your professionalism, and boost your confidence.

In the Royal Navy I was given a grant to buy tailor-made uniforms. We were offered the choice of a number of tailors. What was surprising was the difference in quality when the uniforms had to be of the same design. I chose the leading firm of Gieves and Hawkes of Number One Saville Row, London, whose craftsmanship and materials are the finest in the world. A big investment at the time, but one I was to be very pleased I made. Gieves and Hawkes are now best known for their business suits and quality gentlemen's clothing.

Remember it is the small things that count. Looking like a successful person will bring you one step closer to being a successful person.

SUMMARY

Not all unsolicited mail is junk. Learn from junk mail. What catches your eye, what do you read, and what do you throw in the bin? Think about what you need to do to make people interested in your marketing letters and materials.

Create good filing systems by doing the following:

- ❏ Consider scanning documents and storing them electronically.
- ❏ Try to keep a clear desk and get your employees to do the same.
- ❏ Create a system to deal with incoming mail and stick to it.
- ❏ Conduct planned periodical clear-outs.

WORDS OF WISDOM

When I was at school I learned some valuable lessons that have kept me in good stead:

Life is not fair – the good guys don't always win.

It is not how good you are that matters – it is how good others think you are.

When you set out across an ocean in your small yacht, you do your best to plan for every conceivable eventuality. In business you need to do the same. Always have a Plan B, Plan C, and Plan D. If your path is blocked, look for alternative routes. You need to have gritty determination and strong survival instincts. Remember that you have not failed until you go bust or give up. Never give up, look at adversity as a challenge to overcome, and keep the faith. Look for opportunities and positives in all the trials and tribulations you face. Hold true to your values, maintain your faith, and seek help from anyone prepared to help. Remember yachtswoman Ellen MacArthur: "where there is a will, there is a way." Adversity is a part of business and if you can't cope with it you shouldn't be in business. It is not going to be easy, but that is half the fun.

It can be lonely at the top. Your staff and customers will look to you for reassurance and answers and you must be prepared to give them. Great leaders are made in times of adversity, not times of plenty.

REAL-LIFE STORY

In the early 1990s I set up a new business called the Outdoor Boat and Leisure Show, which was exactly what its name suggested. The first year was highly successful with 3000 visitors, a lovely sunny day, where exhibitors and attendees all seemed to have a good time. The next year the show was expanded, more money was spent on advertising and promotion, and expectations were high. World famous yachtswoman, Ellen MacArthur, came to open the show, which was sponsored by a very large regional newspaper that printed 10,000 show edition copies with a front page entirely dedicated to the show. What I failed to appreciate was that the show coincided with a football cup final. Many exhibitors cancelled at the last minute, a tiny proportion of the expected number of visitors arrived and the number of exhibitors disappointed them. On one side I had angry customers and on the other I had seriously angry exhibitors demanding their money back. I can assure you it was a very uncomfortable experience. My business partner could not cope with the stress and abandoned ship, leaving me to deal with the dissatisfied people. We had acted in good faith, invested considerable amounts of money, and fulfilled our contractual and legal obligations. This disaster, nevertheless, proved to be the last nail in the coffin for the Outdoor Boat and Leisure Show, which never ran again.

I believe it is important to have clear values of honesty and integrity and to act as professionally as you possibly can. Whenever something goes wrong, which it undoubtedly will no matter how good you are, learn from the experience. You have to stand and be counted and face the music no matter how much you would like to run away.

BUSINESS REFIT

The business world advances relentlessly. Like the ocean tides, the business tides never stop changing. A ship has a hard life plying its trade around the world, exposed to the rigors of the seas. It is not surprising that equipment wears out or becomes dated. Because of increased competition, ships undergo refits that update their systems and equipment to maintain their reliability and improve efficiencies. The officers and crew take refresher courses or learn new equipment or techniques.

Your business and employees may also need maintaining and upgrading from time to time. Business application software can be out of date before you have even finished implementing it. New technologies like the Internet and e-mail have to be adopted if you wish to remain competitive.

Not only is there more change in the business world, but also the rate of change seems to continually increase. Past changes were often step changes. In the future, successful companies will need to adjust to the new world conditions of continual change, where advancement is more akin to a ramp than a step, perhaps a series of much smaller steps.

Business improvement should be planned just like ships refit. The worst-case scenario is a breakdown and the need for an unplanned refit. This costs more, takes more time, and gives your competitors a chance to seize advantage.

USE ALL THE FREE RESOURCES AVAILABLE TO YOU

Contrary to popular belief some things in life are free. The business world is full of free energy and resources for you to use if you know where to look. As your ship sets sail, make use of the prevailing currents and winds to assist your passage. Use the predictability of weather patterns to seek favorable conditions. In the summer months the strong "mistral" winds of France and the Meltemi winds of Greece blow off the land. On hot summer days the land sea breezes create onshore winds during the daytime and offshore winds during the night. The daily tidal streams run like clockwork, use them to effect and you can halve your journey times, yet fight them and you can double your journey times. Living in such a technologically advanced world, many people would be surprised to learn that the fastest nonstop voyage around the world was made by a sailing boat and not a motor boat, which used nothing but the free power of the wind and currents. By contrast motorboats can't carry enough fuel to get all the way around the world, and if they can, the weight of the fuel is so heavy that they can't go fast.

In the business world there are similar possibilities. Ride in your competitors' slipstreams, let them advertise and create demand for you to fulfill. Set up next to them so they can draw customers to your business — you don't mind taking their leftovers. Get other people to sell for you as commission-only agents. Legally copy your competitors' best ideas. Take government grants to set up and grow your business. Use viral marketing to let others do the hard work for you. Make use of the free information available in libraries, newspapers, and magazines. Let others do some of your research. Generate PR stories to let others pay for your advertising. There are free rides all over the place if you look hard enough.

BUSINESS OPERATIONS ROOMS — BUSINESS NERVE CENTERS

Modern warships have operations rooms from which the ship can be controlled and the battles fought. In warfare situations the captain

and the principal warfare officer are based in the operations center, from which information is gathered and assessed and actions taken. All the ships sensors such as radar and sonar feed information into powerful computers, which present the information in structured formats. Advanced communications systems are used to share information between ships and aircraft over vast areas. Life-critical decisions have to be made within seconds and the command and control systems need to be good. Imagine an incoming missile flying at supersonic speeds towards you, just ten seconds to impact — nine, eight, seven — what are you going to do? Six, launch anti-missile missiles, five, four, three, two, engage goalkeeper defense systems, one, enemy missile destroyed. You might imagine that naval warfare is just about white-knuckle situations like this, but the reality is that combat is preceded by hours, days, and weeks of strategy and tactics, supported by years of systems development, planning, and scenario modeling. It is more akin to three-dimensional chess than anything else. Actual combat is relatively short-lived and comes at the final stages of complex strategies and tactics. These days' politics play a major role in military operations.

The similarities with the business world are striking, long-range planning, new products brought to development, marketing and branding, and sales. Both play games to win. Each fights battles of one sort or another. The objectives might be different, but both have purpose. Use organizations, systems, resources and people to achieve results. Naval captains and captains of industry share many of the same challenges.

All businesses need intelligence from whatever sources are available, and they need to assess information and make decisions based upon it. Successful companies use management insight and management information.

Imagine if it were possible to bring together all the key sources of business information (key performance indicators) into a central executive control room. Imagine, too, if this information could be used to create numerous "what if" scenarios to look at what actions would deliver the best results, and then controls and settings adjusted to fine-tune the organization's operation. Finally, imagine if it were possible to learn by analysis of actual results and predict likely outcomes and scenarios.

A business is just a giant system with lots of components all working together to deliver shareholder value. I believe that high tech business control rooms for executives will become "must haves" for the future, allowing business leaders to reduce margins of error and increase the responsiveness of their businesses.

THE CAUSE AND EFFECT MYSTERY

As the leader of your business, you can make an infinite number of choices and take an infinite number of actions, which will all impact your business success. It could be argued therefore that you are totally responsible for the failure or success of your business. The degree of success is not only a result of your choices and actions, but also the choices and actions of others and circumstances or conditions completely outside your control.

Given that business success or failure is measured in shareholder value, how can you know for sure which choices and actions most impacted the result? If you look at any business newspaper, you will most likely see business executives claiming credit for delivering outstanding results and blaming market conditions or other factors that are outside their control for poor results.

It is important that you try to discover why you have successes and why you have failures so you can focus most of your attention on things that have the greatest positive influence.

Some big corporate leaders have gotten to the top by fast-track career advancement within their organizations, claiming credit for successes generated by others and moving on soon enough to blame their successors for subsequent failures. Anyone who works in a big corporation has seen examples of this.

....

WORDS OF WISDOM

It is often not how good you are that matters, it is how good people think you are - perception is reality.

....

Be an ice breaker

"Breaking the ice" is a term used to describe getting started. It is normally used in context with relationships, getting to know someone, making introductions and interacting.

Many people are shy or nervous when it comes to meeting new people. Salesmen who are usually one of the most outgoing types of people are sometimes fearful of picking up the phone to call a new prospect. They sometimes dread walking into a company where they know no one.

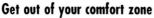

The cause of this is fear of rejection and fear of the unknown. None of us likes to be rejected. Even though it might be in a business context, it can feel highly personal. We are human beings, and we are subject to emotions and feelings that influence our lives significantly.

Get out of your comfort zone

We all have comfort zones. When we step outside our comfort zone, we can feel terrified or anxious. This is fear of the unknown. When we leave our comfort zones, we leave the familiar. The more we are outside our comfort zones, the more uncertainty we have about the outcome. We can feel vulnerable and see our confidence levels drop and our behavior change. An example might be to be asked onto stage at a company conference to make a speech you haven't prepared or weren't expecting. In front of your work colleagues with the spotlight and everyone's attention on you, you could be forgiven for feeling uncomfortable. Your mind spins, you can't think what to say, and your words come out wrong. Physically your heart beats faster, you feel conscious of your own breathing and you might start a nervous sweat.

Lead from the front

As a business leader, lead by example. Help your employees feel more confident and at ease. Your business needs to break a lot of ice. You need to make new contacts, form new relationships, and face a few rejections.

New business comes from new customers and, as such, you don't know them. Someone has to break the ice, introduce him or herself and your company, and ask for business. Even generating new sales from existing customers might mean getting to know new people in different departments. If you have an introduction, it will be easier and you are less likely to be rejected, more likely to know a little about them.

 You can break the ice for your organization in a number of different ways, two of which are:

1. Join local trade organizations and network.
2. Join industry organizations and network.

Make a point of writing five letters a week to new customers to introduce yourself. Follow up with a phone call.

Find reasons to make contact so you have reasons to get in touch, e.g., letters of congratulation for companies winning awards, letters to companies that have appeared in the local newspapers, people mentioned in trade journals who have moved into new jobs, companies that are relocating to the area — welcome them. Make other peoples' business your business.

THE IMPORTANCE OF THE TRUTH

Truth is a vital concept in business — it is the reality, the indisputable fact. As a business leader you need to understand why you and your business are successful or not. While being wildly successful is wonderful, you should be very concerned if you don't know why. Past success is no guarantee of future success. There are examples of this everywhere such as Enron and Arthur Andersen.

It is easy to think you know why you are successful, but can you prove it? It is equally important to know what went wrong, so you can learn from the experience and not repeat the same mistakes. This way you get a positive from every negative.

Beware the hazards of misinformation

As a business leader, you have a dilemma when seeking the truth in knowing who or what to believe. You will be presented with

information continually from employees, suppliers, customers, and advisers. You must understand that their interests are often very different from yours, despite what they might show or what outward appearances may suggest.

Beware of majority opinion, it may well be wrong. Many of the decisions and actions you take may be unpopular. It is natural to expect resistance, but remember that resistance comes in many forms, perhaps support to your face and sabotage behind your back. Some people will have a vested interest in making sure your ideas don't work or that even if they do, they might try to suggest that they don't.

It can be lonely at the top. You want to be able to make decisions and actions based on correct information. Sometimes you will need to act on intuition and trust your own judgment. It is dangerous to bury your head in the sand and think you are always right, but it is equally dangerous to act against your own better judgment on the say-so of others.

This is a tricky issue. Be honest with yourself at all times. The truth starts with you and it is important to recognize when you are right and when you are wrong. Question and challenge yourself continually, and look for impartial advice from others you can trust, as well as those you don't. Look for consensus of opinion from those unconnected parties.

....

WORDS OF WISDOM
It is better to pause and think than act in haste without thought.
....

BUSINESS STAGES

Business is not for the faint-hearted. Things are not always what they appear to be. Business can be likened to TV soaps where the participants are acting their business roles. The facades of the sets may look good, but there isn't necessarily substance behind them. For some, business stages may include:

- Enthusiasm

- Disillusionment

- Panic

- Search for the guilty

- Punishment of the innocent

- Praise and honor for the nonparticipants

....

WORDS OF WISDOM

Don't be surprised by anything –
if it can happen it possibly
will.

....

REWARD AND RECOGNITION

Rewards can come in all shapes and sizes. When we first talk of reward, our natural instinct is to think of financial rewards, salary, benefits, packages, perks, etc. Rewards may also be enjoyment, satisfaction, challenge, development, friendship, belonging, or personal growth. Why do so many people do charity work? Is it because they are so rich they don't need financial rewards? In most cases, probably not. Most likely they are driven by a higher purpose, a satisfaction about helping others. Earlier I identified that I believed just three things make people happy:

1. Having something to look forward to

2. Making other people happy

3. Sharing

How rewarding it is to make others happy. Any parent will instantly recognize the pleasure they receive from making their own children happy.

In the business environment, it's important to think hard about what rewards you seek yourself and what rewards would motivate others around you. I believe time is our most precious asset and companies would do well to use it as a means of reward such as extra vacation time, paid days off, and shorter workdays, which might provide greater rewards than any financial incentive. Flexibility is a great reward in itself. How much more flexible could you be with your employees? When considering rewards, you may be surprised at what you come up with when you think outside the box.

 Reward is one side of motivation. Recognition, which is frequently ignored, is the other. A "thank you" for a job well done costs nothing, but it can have a positive impact on motivation. We all need to feel valued and as business leaders, it is our job to make others feel valued.

Carrot and stick

It is commonly recognized that rewards and punishments (carrot and stick) motivate people. A donkey might respond to a carrot and stick, but human beings are far more complex.

THE BUSINESS/PEOPLE/TECHNOLOGY TRIANGLE

The business objectives define the purpose, where you are going, and what you are intending to achieve. The strategy, organization, structure, processes and methods, policies and procedures, controls, performance measures, etc. support the achievement of the business objectives. Technology is a tool, which helps you to achieve your business objectives. People are the deciding factors in whether you will achieve your business objectives or not.

THE PEOPLE FACTOR

People undoubtedly are responsible for successful and unsuccessful companies. They may be your greatest assets or your greatest liabilities. The trick is to get extraordinary performance from ordinary people.

To get extraordinary performance out of ordinary people, you can learn some lessons from the military, which were discussed earlier in this book. You can also look to systemize your business in the same way as large successful companies. People's positions should be well thought out, with clearly defined roles that are clearly communicated. Good training and management communication is critical. Incentive and penalty mechanisms should be put in place to encourage and reinforce the behavior and performance you desire.

The "can't get good people" phenomenon

How often do you hear business people say, "I can't get good people?" Quite often I expect. Everyone has his or her own definition of "good." Remember, good people are only human, too, and they are good only up until the last time they were! Few people are going to readily admit they are bad, yet the actions and performance of many certainly point in that direction. Many people live off successes that happened a long time ago or possibly never happened at all. You are never likely to get a bad reference when you hire someone.

People are expensive to employ, costly to train, and subject to failures more often than most machines. People need good management and clear leadership, which is sometimes very hard to provide. Circumstances are rarely ideal, which means the challenge to get the best from them is great.

 As human beings, we all respond to the way we are treated. Treat us well, be kind, caring, and supportive, and the likelihood is we will reciprocate. Treat us badly and we may well respond in kind. As a business leader, the way you treat people directly correlates to the performance you will see from them.

Getting the most from people

❑ Treat others, as you would expect to be treated yourself.

❑ Be prepared to do anything you ask others to do.

❑ Create an environment where your employees are set up to succeed not fail.

❑ Be fair, but firm when necessary.

❑ Set and expect high standards; people will respect them.

❑ Reward achievement, not effort.

❑ Help your staff to develop themselves.

❑ Work with each employee to provide career progression — we all need to move up the escalator of life.

❑ Consider things from your employees' perspective and do what it takes to make their life easier, without compromising business success.

❑ Set an example yourself.

Avoiding mutiny

You should never forget that business is a game and there are winners and losers at almost every level. It is easy to think of the major threats as external, yet the greatest threats business leaders might face could be internal.

People commonly talk about politics at work. This happens in most companies, even very small ones. It is all part of the internal business game. There are some people who will do anything to advance their position, e.g., lie, cheat, sabotage someone else, stab a coworker in the back. Anyone who has been involved in business for some time will most likely have seen some evidence of this. Business is a microcosm of society. Everything that happens in society as a whole can happen in business, so be prepared and remain vigilant.

No employee should have too big a part of your customers

Imagine a situation where one of your employees holds the entire relationship with your customer. If they leave and set up their own business, you may well find customers leave you too. Even if your ex-employees don't set out to compete or try to entice away your customers, you may well find that they work for one of your competitors and your customers gravitate to them of their own free will.

It is often said "people deal with people," which they will, given half a chance. Even if your business is a service business there is no reason why the customer can't deal with different people all the time and still have a good relationship with your business. Bigger companies make it a practice to create a corporate entity that stands on its own regardless of the individuals who work in it. These practices might include branding, conformity of uniforms, service, training, or structured processes and controls. Some businesses are much more susceptible to "relationship hijacking" than others. For example, women's hair stylists and consultants in small firms are often individual relationship-dependent. Don't let your business be taken hostage.

Always look for ways to spread the customer relationship among as many of your employees as possible. Customers should be able to see clearly that it doesn't matter who works for your company, they can still rely on the same level of quality, service, and experience.

Why one-man bands can't grow and don't want to grow

Some might suggest lack of funds, excessive legislation, and regulation are the primary causes that small one-man businesses can't grow or don't want to grow. I think the real reason is they simply don't want to employ other people.

Ask any business leader what causes the most headaches and it is quite likely the answer will be people problems. Employing people can be a pain in the backside; they can be expensive, demanding, difficult, challenging, and temperamental. They are guaranteed to take but not guaranteed to give, they need regular supervision, cost a lot, and don't always do what you want them to do.

There is a fundamental difference between businesses where owners do most of the work themselves and businesses that rely on most of the work being done by other people. It is a very different world trying to get things done through others. They never seem to do things as well or as reliably as you the business leader. They may complain, want sick pay, holiday pay, and attractive benefits and perks before they have contributed anything.

Managing people and getting work done through others is one of the most difficult things any business leader has to achieve. There are no set rules, every situation is different, and you are guaranteed staff headaches from time to time.

TECHNOLOGY AS A CATALYST FOR BUSINESS IMPROVEMENT

Since earliest times, technology has been a major catalyst for business change because it offers competitive advantage. If we consider manufacturing businesses, it is easy to see how the introduction of new or better machines increases productivity, quality, and reduces unit costs.

New technology in most cases represents progress, an unstoppable phenomenon.

Technology has applications in almost every conceivable business context. It can help to improve operational efficiency and reduce cost. Technology replaces people. People cost money and are often considerably less reliable.

If we look back to the last century, it is possible to see patterns in the invention and adoption of technology. For example, a hundred years ago who had a telephone? Seventy-five years ago who had a wireless? Fifty years ago who had a TV? Twenty years ago who had a fax machine? Ten years ago who had a mobile phone? Five years ago who had a Web site? The reality is that new technology is arriving all the time. It represents the progress that cannot be stopped or ignored.

Technology offers the potential for differentiation and differentiation means competitive advantage. I believe it could be argued that technology inventors create the problem in the first place, i.e., the potential for differentiation, and then set themselves up as the solution. Whatever you believe, technology represents either a threat or an opportunity or both. Ignore it at your peril!

Three key technological areas to affect the business world in recent times are Enterprise Resource Planning (ERP), and Customer Relationship Management (CRM), and e-commerce. Enterprise resource planning focused on integrating business computer systems to manage back office functional areas including production planning, materials management, sales and distribution/supply chain, financial control, human resources, etc. Customer relationship management focuses on the front office areas of sales, marketing, service and support. Enterprise resource planning is intended to deliver primarily cost savings while CRM is intended to primarily increase sales revenues. Enterprise resource planning as a technology and concept was linked to business process re-engineering (BPR) where the implementation of new technology was used as a catalyst to improve processes throughout entire corporations. These processes would involve those carried out by computers and by people.

The concept of ERP and CRM are very logical and fundamentally right. The problem has been in finding ways to successfully implement them and manage the resultant changes within the business. These issues have been so difficult for business managers to fully understand that they have relied heavily on external consultants to advise them. Those consultants have been predominantly biased towards the technology elements of the concepts. As a result, admitted failure rates are extremely high and in the case of customer relationship management, research has shown that in eighty percent of cases, expected benefits had not been achieved. In my opinion, it has been a case of the blind leading the blind. I admit I have been a part of these industries that failed our customers.

Technology sheep syndrome

Despite commercial pressures and the need for competitive advantage, most business leaders are followers. There are very few pure entrepreneurs. True entrepreneurs are those who invent and create concepts, products, and services for others to adopt and follow. There is a continuous cycle few are aware of whereby new concepts arrive in the business world in clearly defined themes. Technology is by far the biggest driver but is not the exclusive driver.

For example, fax machine technology arrived, faxes replaced the telex, and now virtually all businesses, even the smallest, have to have a fax machine. Likewise, mobile phone technology arrived and now few of us are without them. In the world of large corporations, enterprise resource planning and business process re-engineering arrived, and nearly all the players dutifully followed suit. As this market became saturated and demand started to drop, the customer relationship management market was born with a corresponding number of large corporations following each other to adopt the new technology and concepts. In smaller companies, computerized accounting systems arrived and small companies dutifully adopted them. Most remarkable, perhaps, was the arrival of the Internet and e-commerce, which swept through the global business world and created the dot-com bubble.

It is absolutely common for new concepts to be over-inflated, over-hyped, and to eventually burst in one way or another. What is interesting is that new industries have been created around the concept of new business concepts. Someone creates a new concept and financiers pour huge sums of money into these businesses. The new concepts offer competitive advantage that is irresistible to the business market. Finance is used for product and service development, but also sophisticated sales and marketing campaigns, which are successful. A grateful media industry has arisen to support the new concepts, comprising industry publications, technology publications, and business publications, etc. There is also an education industry, which makes hay while the sun shines on the new business concepts. Look out for new courses, seminars, and books. The mass of media coverage fuels a demand frenzy that provides considerable revenue for technology vendors, their business partners, and associated industries. Once the snowball starts to roll down the hill there is no stopping it.

If your competitors are adopting the concepts, you feel compelled to follow suit and you feel reassured that you are not alone in buying into the new ideas. In fact, you may want to lead, gaining competitive advantage yourself. If adopting a new technology can cut costs by ten percent, that is great. But if it cuts your competitors' costs by ten percent also, you are not much better off. Market forces will drive margins down so the net effect might not be any different. If you are able to gain short-term advantage then that might be worthwhile. By doing nothing you may well lose out. You might, therefore, have to invest just to maintain the status quo.

Many of the biggest technology vendors and global professional services organizations have lost the trust and confidence of their customers, who are now highly suspicious — although not totally disinterested — in the latest concepts. The commercial pressures of competitive advantage continue to apply regardless of failed concepts along the way.

I believe in most cases the concept is absolutely right and the failure has resulted from the solution, which has been predominantly a technology product and its implementation. The technology product has been regarded as the solution rather than just a component of the solution. You need to ensure that you are not fooled and that you do not become a victim of the sheep syndrome.

The truth about business application software

Few business people would doubt the value of business application software, yet few know that according to the well-respected Gartner Group research "approximately seventy percent of IT-related projects fail to deliver the expected benefits." Companies frequently buy software on emotion or on a follow-the-leader basis and cost/benefit analysis isn't done before purchasing. If you don't know what benefits you expect to get and you have no means of measuring it, you are going to remain in the dark forever.

Ignorance is bliss?

Few of us would like to think of ourselves as ignorant, but when it comes to technology we are conditioned by a market to trust the software vendors and implementers and to put our faith in the products. Benefits don't just magically happen; you have to make them happen.

IT people understand the technology and business people understand the business. Understanding how to get the technology to serve the business effectively is incredibly difficult. In the majority of cases the business people think the technology is serving the business and are unaware of how much better they could be served. If one used an analogy of a car, it is like having a powerful sports car, where the engine is only producing fifty percent of the potential power. If you are a businessperson (driver) and haven't experienced full power, then you don't know what you are missing. Even if you do you might think you need a more powerful car, when in fact you need to fix the engine you already have. If the IT people are the mechanics and technicians, they understand the technology, but they don't do any driving. They have to rely on the drivers to tell them what's happening. The problems are obvious.

The answers are of course that the drivers have got to learn about the technology and the technologists have got to learn how to drive to understand what the drivers want and need. This is easier said than done, due to work pressures, interest, and aptitude.

The 80/20 rule

Software functionality is expensive. Generally speaking the greater the software's capability the more it costs to buy. Research shows that frequently customers use approximately twenty percent of their software's capability.

The major benefits frequently come from ten percent or less of a system's functionality. Learning to understand and use software functionality is expensive. The more functionality you have to learn, the longer it takes and the more likely you are to forget.

Companies waste billions of dollars every year buying complex, expensive systems when cheaper, simpler ones would have done the job just as well, would have taken a fraction of the time to implement and learn.

Do you get what you pay for?

There can be few markets where it is possible to bamboozle customers with clever marketing, technical talk, and industry hype. Business software is one that has successfully managed to do this.

Private disaster stories are everywhere, yet few make it public. Many of the largest business software vendors have faced huge claims from dissatisfied customers; some indeed have been accused of driving companies into bankruptcy.

Do you understand the shelf life of your business software?

Business software has a shelf life. It is like food that goes bad. It doesn't stop working, but it becomes undesirable as newer and better alternatives appear.

It is like having a new car with all the latest features. It's great when you buy it, but four or five years later, there are other new cars with enhanced, better features and performance. Your car still works but in business, performance is everything. There are competitive pressures, and that means differences matter a lot.

Who is working for whom?

Are you working for the software or is it working for you? Are you a slave to data input. Does the data you input actually get used and does it add any value? If so, how much? Equally, does the system save you time or does it cost you time?

Frequently the people inputting the data get no direct benefit from it. It takes valuable time, and that costs money. Marketing, accounting, or management often use data, but sometimes it is hardly used at all. Ownership is blurred, often no thanks go to the real workers, who see no incentive in entering the data or making sure it is accurate and correct.

Business application software can reduce efficiency and increase costs dramatically if you allow it to.

Business application software needs maintaining

There is a false perception among business customers that software is perfect, that it does everything it says it should all of the time. The reality is that it isn't and it doesn't. It often fails miserably, breaks down, or simply doesn't do what you think it should.

You can buy a Rolls Royce or a top-of-the-line Mercedes and expect trouble-free driving. The reality is, however, that you have to maintain it to keep it from breaking down or to keep it working properly and, just occasionally, it might break down anyway. Software is no different; in fact, it is arguably far less reliable than a car, due to its complexity.

There is of course, good and bad software, but even the best software is capable of breaking down or not doing what it is supposed to. Commercial pressures and technical difficulties mean that most software is sold with faults the software vendor is aware of. Even when they sell it without knowing about faults, customers usually manage to find the faults for them. Most faults aren't mission critical, but some are. If you can't create an invoice, take an order, or place a purchase order, you can have big problems.

Set in place the following procedures to circumvent these faults:

- ❏ Planned maintenance
- ❏ Preventative maintenance
- ❏ Breakdown planning
- ❏ Contingency planning

PERSONALITY-BASED MARKETING: THE NEW FRONTIER

Marketing is half science and half art. Understanding customer needs is paramount, yet it is often not enough. Prospects can be categorized into many different segments to establish their likely needs, by questioning and asking them directly with market research. You can even consider their transaction history of

what they have previously purchased to establish what they might wish to purchase in the future. Together these techniques might enable you to establish customer needs very accurately. You might even establish they have the money and are satisfied with the price.

Regrettably, this is not enough to guarantee purchase. Even though you may have the ideal product or service at the ideal price, at the ideal time, in the ideal location, customers are not totally predicable. They are human beings, with their own minds and personalities, capable of making their own choices influenced by their own conscious or subconscious criteria.

Working out what customers want and need is now an every day part of business. Customer databases and recorded transactional information is giving managers greater than ever customer insight.

The last major frontier of marketing is to understand the vagaries of human beings. Why don't they always do what we expect them to do? Surely this is the multi-billion-dollar question. What difference would it make if we could segment personalities and understand the vagaries and varieties of human beings, and use this knowledge to our advantage? An impossible task some might say, but leading psychologists claim to be able to segment humans by personality types. It may seem far-fetched, but it's much closer to reality than you might think.

The development of psychological profiling of the past decade is slowly transforming the world of personal development and HR. The military too have understood the importance of psychological profiling for many years and have used it as part of their recruitment and selection process. Complete some psychological profile tests yourself and you may feel like you are looking in a mirror. They are easy to trash and dismiss until you see the profiles for yourself and see how accurate they can be.

While every person is unique, our personalities do fall into identifiable categories. The characteristics of these different personality types are remarkably similar. It is possible to establish how someone communicates and likes to receive communication, how they are best able to learn, what they are good at and not good at, what things are important to them, and even their life purpose.

The potential is to be able to offer the same thing to different personality types in different ways. Some people may like inspirational pictures, others facts and figures; some people like flowery words and others like bullet points.

What difference would it make to your business if you could increase the success rate of your sales and marketing efforts by even ten or twenty percent? ASAP Institute is pioneering research in this exciting area. If you are interested in sponsoring and participating in this research, e-mail **research@asapinstitute.com**.

CUSTOMER RELATIONSHIP MANAGEMENT

Customer Relationship Management is a hot business issue. Why is it? Could it be that the business and technology media have made it one? The truth is Customer Relationship Management is as old as trading itself.

Customer Relationship Management has become a multi-billion dollar industry. It may be that CRM, as a business concept, has become a fad that serves the purposes of technology, consulting groups, and education and training industries that require change and hot new issues to survive.

The things you should know

Approximately sixty-five percent of CRM implementations fail and that is likely to rise to eighty percent according to Gartner.

The CRM Industry could be accused of causing the business problem, then holding itself up as the solution. My view is that everything in business is relative and it is differences that matter most. Customer perception is the reality that matters. It is not how good you are that matters, it is how good people think you are. In any highly competitive industry, if one company improves its CRM capabilities resulting in competitive advantage, then other companies in the industry are forced to follow suit or suffer the consequences. This point is not just valid for CRM, but equally applies to any new business improvement concept such as, ERP, which was big throughout the nineties. Ten years ago few companies had Web sites; now few companies don't have them.

Business improvement benefits can be self-canceling, e.g., you succeed in reducing your cost of sales by ten percent and, therefore, make ten percent more. If your competitors do the same, it is highly unusual that you both make ten percent more. Competitive forces normally kick in and the customers end up being the sole beneficiaries, creating a win/lose situation for your business.

Customer Relationship Management is just another business concept that is flowing through the corporate world. As soon as it loses steam, another concept will be invented to provide a livelihood for the technology and consultancy industries.

The only constant is change — the certainty that there will always be something new around the corner. Remember:

- Technology is often the catalyst, but the issues are mostly business ones.

- Technology frequently provides the greatest opportunities, but also presents the greatest threats.

- Each new technology fad such as CRM spurns experts, jargon, and fabrication in copious quantities.

CRM is such a complex issue to fully understand that installing computer software is the easiest thing to do, yet you will not see the benefits unless people, process, structure, organization, and attitudes are addressed, not simply as a one-off exercise, but on an ongoing basis.

Information overload

There is now so much information and so many opinions about CRM, each slightly different, it is difficult to see the forest for the trees. Who should you believe and trust? Where should you seek impartial advice? There is no internationally accepted central body responsible for CRM, no global standards, assessments, or accreditation. In fact, there are no barriers to entry; the market is as open to real masters as it is to con men. As a customer, how can you possibly tell the difference?

The key market drivers are the software companies, with massive budgets. They frequently sell through business partners who deliver services and complimentary products. Supporting these is a mass of support companies, marketing and advertising companies, business and trade press, exhibition and conference organizers, etc.

Follow your judgment and common sense

Remember CRM is not new; we all practice it anyway, often without even thinking about it. Seek advice and knowledge by all means, but trust only yourself.

All software has bugs and will go wrong sometimes. Software failure is not a question of if, but when!

CRM is about business not technology

You are doomed to failure if you think CRM is about technology. It is just a tool, an enabler to business improvement.

Understand your business objectives before considering CRM

It might sound obvious, but knowing what you want your business to achieve should be the starting point of any CRM improvement project. Most people would say they want to increase their company's sales, reduce their costs, and maximize their profits. In fact, who wouldn't?

General objectives are the least likely ones to be achieved. They are, by nature, open-ended and are frequently described as "Maximize" or "As much as possible." If you are considering CRM, you should have a clearly documented, quantitative CRM vision for your company.

CRM objectives

In the simplest form, companies do just two things: buy and sell. They buy goods or services and sell them. The trick is to make a profit. In simple terms, the way companies do this is to make sure they sell for a greater price than the price they pay when they buy. There are obviously costs associated with running a business and these, too, need to be taken into account.

To make more profit, there are only two things you can do:

1. Increase your sales revenues.

2. Reduce your costs.

To increase your sales revenues there are only three things that you can do:

1. Win new customers.

2. Keep your existing customers.

3. Do more business with all customers.

Ask yourself these questions to determine what your high-level CRM objectives should be:

- ❑ How much do you want to increase your sales revenues over a given time?

- ❑ How much do you want to reduce your costs over a given time?

- ❑ How do you want to balance costs and sales revenues? (Costs might rise, but sales revenues and profitability might rise proportionately higher. A consequence of increased sales is increased costs.)

CRM to gain competitive advantage or to defend against business threats?

It is nice to think about businesses going onwards and upwards, but the reality is that sometimes industries shrink and companies have to shrink with them. In defensive situations investment in CRM might just limit the amount of fall in sales revenue or profits or the rise in costs.

Your CRM objectives are personal to your company

Business is immensely complex and most companies' situations are unique to them. Creating clear and measurable CRM objectives is more difficult than it seems. Not having them or having poor or unclear objectives is probably the greatest reason that most CRM projects fail.

Can you afford to ignore CRM?

There are some circumstances where CRM has little impact; however, in ninety-nine percent of the cases CRM is not only important, it is the very lifeblood of the company.

How to be smart with CRM

- Be first.
- Be better.
- Concentrate efforts on things that deliver the greatest returns.

How to judge CRM capabilities

- Understand who customers are.
- Understand what relationships you have with customers.
- Weight importance.

What are the elements of CRM?

1. **Marketing:** Attracting customers and doing more business with existing customers
2. **Sales:** Winning new customers and doing more business with existing customers
3. **Service:** Keeping existing customers and doing more business with existing customers
4. **Support:** Keeping existing customers

What are CRM capabilities?

 Capabilities are the ability to do. When considering your CRM capabilities, ask yourself the following questions:

- ❏ What can I do?
- ❏ How easy am I to do business with?
- ❏ How can I be contacted?
- ❏ How do I generate enquires?
- ❏ How do I deal with enquires?
- ❏ How do I provide information?
- ❏ What are my response times?
- ❏ What do I do relative to my competitors?
- ❏ How do customers see me?
- ❏ What do customers want?
- ❏ What would it take to meet customers' expectations?
- ❏ How often do customers' expectations change?
- ❏ How many customer contacts do I have per customer per annum?
- ❏ How many contacts are active and how many passive?
- ❏ How do I solicit customer feedback?
- ❏ How do I incorporate feedback and make changes?
- ❏ Who in my customers' companies do I have a relationship with?
- ❏ What is it like to be one of my customers?
- ❏ How do I cope with staff change?
- ❏ How interested are my customers in me?

WORDS OF WISDOM

Talk and words are cheap. It is actions that matter.

Concentrate on the outcomes, not on the inputs.

Not many people can "Walk the talk."

Learn to recognize when customers are customers and when they are ex-customers.

Understanding the benefits of investing in CRM and ROI

There is no point investing in CRM unless you know what benefits you expect to receive in doing so.

If you don't think there are any, then don't invest, but if you think there are benefits, quantify what they are, place a financial value on them, and compare them to the cost of the investment.

What are customer relationships?

Legal: Buyer and seller relationship

Emotional: Brand values, familiarity, well-known

Personal: Person-to-person

What are you managing?

What are you managing, the customer or the relationship? What happens if a customer doesn't want to be managed? Can you manage a relationship with someone who doesn't want a relationship? Can a relationship be solely one-sided? These are all questions you need to answer.

The people factor is the most important CRM missing link

Technology is beautifully and carefully packaged, its functionality is clearly defined, and the marketing is usually very impressive. It is hardly surprising, therefore, that most companies wishing to implement CRM turn very quickly to the software suppliers. Most CRM vendors market their products via a reseller network that usually provides services to support the implementation of the software.

Most CRM software vendors and resellers readily acknowledge that there is more to CRM than software, yet offer little of substance to help customers address the non-technology part of CRM.

Companies are run and controlled by people. Whether you are buying or selling, there are ultimately people at either end. In a B2C environment, the customer is an individual and easy to identify. In a B2B environment, customers are businesses, and with the exception of sole proprietors, and partnerships, businesses are limited liability companies. A corporation is effectively a legal entity. By definition, a legal entity is an inert legal structure that, on its own, does nothing, doesn't think, and doesn't have feelings or emotions. People make companies do things. If your customer is a company, think about with whom in the company you have a relationship. In many cases the answers are not clear. What is likely is that you have a fairly complex many-to-many relationship, where sales people deal with buyers, accounts departments deal with accounts departments, directors deal with directors, shipping departments deal with receiving departments, account managers deal with just about everybody, and it can all become awfully complicated. Some people are decision makers, others are influencers, and some are either beneficiaries or casualties of the relationship. There are all sort of different relationships, transactional suppliers, value-added resellers, trusted business partners, one-time suppliers. Whatever the type of relationship, there are always people involved and it is always people who make decisions. Equally, people sell, people serve customers, and people either care or they don't.

 People are the most important element in relationships and, therefore, they should figure highly in any CRM program. The scant regard given to people in most CRM programs is quite remarkable. I would suggest that the lack of focus on people is probably the greatest reason CRM projects fail. In most CRM projects the people focus centers on introducing new technology, how to use the system, and what is happening with the system implementation project.

The basic objectives of any CRM program should surely be to increase sales and profits by winning new customers, keeping your existing ones, doing more business with them, reducing your cost of sales, and increasing your margins. Two of the most important groups in achieving this are sales and customer service.

If you were asked to stake your life on whether installing a new computing system or improving the sales skills of your salesmen was most likely to increase your sales, what would you choose? I would stake my life on increasing the sales skills of the salespeople. If you were asked to choose whether installing a new computer system or improving the customer service skills of a staff that has customer contact, which would you choose? My money would go on the improving the sales and customer service skills of my staff. I have asked these same questions to many people and not one person has come up with an answer different from mine.

Why is it when it comes to investing in business improvement, companies choose installing the computer system almost every time? Could it have something to do with the fact that there is a slick industry selling computer systems and a media industry around it that influence us so much we act against our natural instinct?

Don't fall into the technology versus training trap

When times are tough, typically staff training and development are the first budgets to be cut. Businesses seem prepared to invest huge amounts per head on computer systems, but balk at comparatively modest amounts on training and development. I would like to understand the reasons for this phenomenon. What adds to the situation and makes it more remarkable is that businesses have previously invested in technology and failed to see the expected benefits in things such as ERP, yet are prepared to come back for more technology and believe that this time, things will be different. Even bad media coverage doesn't seem to deter that many companies; everyone thinks it won't happen to me. Though we often despise it, I feel the world has become addicted to technology, that it somehow provides an element of comfort in a fast changing world. If other people are doing it, we feel compelled to follow suit, we don't want to be left behind. We don't want to be accused of being behind the times.

I confess that to an extent, I am guilty of this phenomenon too. I have tried to be very honest with myself and understand why we do this. A few points that come to mind are as follows:

- When you invest in technology, you feel you have something tangible, an asset that remains with the company.

- You may be concerned if you invest in training and development of staff, they might leave and the investment will walk out the door.

- Big technology investments can easily be financed.

- Technology promises rapid improvements.

- Technology seems interesting and exciting.

- Large technology investments are more acceptable to the outside world than large training and development investments.

- You fear that training and development won't actually work.

- You are concerned that with training and development you don't have anything tangible to show for it, and its results seem harder to quantify.

- You are concerned that training people don't live in the real world, they are somehow too far removed.

- Generally speaking, development trainers are seen as inferior to technologists who seem to carry more weight and influence.

- Companies are used to investing more in technology than in training.

- There are time constraints with employees on technology training and development training; sometimes you can't afford to do both.

Technology gives management more visibility and control, while training and development gives management less visibility and control as employees are empowered and possibly need management less. You can't own people but you can own technology. The technology industry is much better at presenting a return on investment case, albeit frequently a work of fiction, than the training and development industry. In the corporate pecking order, IT seems to attract more power than HR, the group that is the traditional owner of training and development.

As an employer you have very little control over employees leaving. You can invest in your employees' training and development, which makes them worth more on the job market. Their newfound sense of self-worth can prompt employees to look for more interesting and better-paying work elsewhere. It is all well and good thinking you can provide a career path and more interesting work. The realities don't always allow that. You can hardly afford to pay them more until you have benefited financially from the investment you have made in them and that might take years, not months.

A good compromise is to openly discuss this issue with employees prior to investing in their training and development. You can agree on the payback period in advance; it is no good trying to address the issue after the event. If employees are encouraged to take out career development loans, the employer can reimburse the employee the cost of the repayment monthly. If the employee leaves, they are faced with paying off the loan themselves. This can be easily done with new employees, but it is not so easy with existing work forces that are less likely to agree to the terms.

RECOVERING DAMAGED CUSTOMER RELATIONSHIPS

HOW TO REPAIR DAMAGE TO A CUSTOMER RELATIONSHIP

Before you can repair damage to a customer relationship, you must first determine:

1. What type of relationship you have with the customer?
   - Personal or impersonal
   - Reseller
   - Valued business partner

2. What is the nature of the damage?
   - Breach of trust
   - Breach of confidence
   - Poor service
   - Missed deadlines
   - Let-down on delivery
   - Interpersonal problems

It takes a long time to build relationships, but they can be destroyed very quickly. In a service business, relationship is everything and is your biggest differentiator. To rebuild the relationship and repair the damage, you need to invest in it. This investment is in time, effort and, of course, money.

To rebuild a damaged relationship means you need to:

❑ Communicate with customer

   1. In writing

   2. By telephone

   3. In person

❑ Investigate and understand, empathize

❑ Give and contribute

   1. Time

   2. Advice and information

   3. Material goods: gifts, lunches, dinners, hospitality

   4. Value: free seminars

❑ Demonstrate

   1. Interest

   2. Understanding

❑ Stay in touch

WORDS OF WISDOM

To repair damaged relationships, you need to work harder than when you create new ones in the first place.

REAL-LIFE STORY

To be a business leader, you don't necessarily need to own your business. In writing this book, I had in mind both people leading small-to medium-sized enterprises or smaller divisions of large corporations.

Many years ago I worked for the Mobil Oil Corporation, which was then the world's fourth largest company. Now called Exxon Mobil Corporation, it remains one of the largest companies on the planet.

I was transfered to a subsidiary called Prime Garages, which operated about two hundred of Mobil's highest volume gasoline stations in the United Kingdom. I was an area manager for twenty stations in Northwest London. My business unit had a turnover of about $20 million and employed about eighty people.

Within a framework of operation, I had total responsibility for the bottom-line profitability of the business unit I managed and also had considerable autonomy to hire and fire and make operational and commercial decisions. My business unit operated 24/7 and for all practical purposes, the buck stopped with me.

I learned that the issues divisions of large corporations face are very similar to those of small, privately-owned businesses. In effect, each of my gasoline stations was a small business. Over time I have realized that divisions of large corporations can learn a lot from small, privately-owned businesses and visa versa.

In just two years I had numerous business experiences, both good and bad. My gas stations experienced no less than five armed robberies, two using guns. One even happened when I was on site marking the car wash for cleanliness. Another time, one of my managers lost the weekend's cash takings, probably $10–20,000, on the way to the bank. We suspected the person concerned had stolen the money himself. Fraud and theft were common in the industry at the time, and only tight controls and rigorous scrutiny checked wrongdoing and prevented more. Perhaps low pay and dire personal circumstances were to blame. I became suspicious of one of my managers and decided to investigate further. By watching his gas station from a distance at night, I discovered he had invented employees who didn't exist and was paying them, or rather, pocketing the money himself. He worked shifts as a cashier and brought his own personal stock, which he sold for cash, depriving the company of its rightful profits. One of my young managers, Fran, who was just twenty-two, died one Christmas in a car accident. She was on her way back from buying some Christmas decorations for her station from a block of shops less than a mile away. Fran was a wonderful person, full of energy and enthusiasm, and her tragic loss was difficult for all her colleagues.

Workers were intimidated by customers, gypsies, and hooligans. Gas stations were vandalized or burgled at night. One night the police camped out in the back office of a station that closed between 11 p.m. and 7 a.m., with the lights turned off. Sure enough, the burglars arrived and broke in only to be caught by the police. Shoplifting and what we called "drive offs," where people filled their cars with gasoline and then drove off without paying, were commonplace. During one violent storm, the wind pressure coming through the shop door blew out the wall-sized window. The gasoline station forecourt looked more like a bombed-out site in Iraq. On another day, a motorist not used to his automatic transmission lunged forward straight through the shop window, pushing the cashiers' counter back two feet.

Some businesses are undoubtedly tough, and this was one of them. Yet in spite of this, I had the honor to work with one of the finest teams I have ever met, people who demonstrated intelligence, courage, determination, and resilience. How some of them coped with the pressures and stresses they were under amazed me. They earned low wages and, even so, had to be on call 24/7.

I have realized that adversity can either bring people together into a tight team, as it did here, or have the opposite effect and bring out the worst in people, which I have seen elsewhere. What might surprise some people is that most actually enjoyed their work. Despite its difficulties, they helped and supported each other. If one person slacked off, he let down the whole team.

On a positive note, my area achieved record sales and profitability, winning the company's annual incentive award. We did have fun and gained some satisfaction from overcoming the hurdles placed in our way.

I think many businesses are difficult, even ones others think are easy. All businesses have their ups and downs, and it takes business leader strength to ride through the storms. The effort to returns ratio can sometimes be very high. This chapter looks at the things they don't teach you in business school. Perhaps these concepts are part of the business facts of life. It is better to learn them in advance and be prepared, rather than discover them the hard way.

This example highlights just some of the challenges that one business faced. What I have realized is that a key secret of success is to obtain extraordinary performance from ordinary people.

Any life ultimately ends in death, and so it is for businesses too.
Fear not the inevitable, but learn to extend your businesses life and know
when to plan for its death. Remember that new beginnings can grow from
the seeds of old businesses. The future is full of possibilities and opportunities,
if you only look hard enough.

CHAPTER 7:
The Business Death

BUSINESS RIP

Sooner or later all businesses will end or become part of other businesses. The business end may be murder, suicide, accidental, or deliberate. Their ending is either voluntary or involuntary. In other words, their owners chose to end them or circumstances or others forced them to end.

Different businesses can have different legal entities, as I mentioned earlier. "The business" means the "trading activity" or purpose. "The business" can be divorced from the legal entity that operates it; in other words, it is possible to buy the business but not the company. This could include customers, goodwill, assets, liabilities, etc.

One hopes that if you are the owner of the business, it will have served you well and given you good shareholder value over its life.

BUSINESS MURDER

Your competitors, previous owners, or even disgruntled ex-employees may try hard to put you out of business, either legally with fair competition or illegally, by trying to harm your reputation or cause damage to your finances.

BUSINESS SUICIDE

You might have over traded, run out of money through poor financial control, or committed corporate fraud. It is clearly your fault your business has ended.

BUSINESS ACCIDENT

You sold some stock in good faith, but ultimately found out the company was dishonest and had gone bankrupt. There was no way you could have anticipated this happening. Perhaps your business is destroyed by an unforeseen natural disaster that is not covered by your insurance.

BUSINESS CLOSURE BY CHOICE

You have had enough, you can't find a buyer, or you may not want a buyer, so you decide to close it down.

BUSINESS MERGER

Two businesses can join together to become a new business.

BUSINESS SPLIT-UP

A business can be split up to form new independent businesses.

BUSINESS LEADER EXIT

Business leaders who have not divorced themselves personally from their business are likely to cause it significant harm if or when they leave. Over-dependency on the business leader should be avoided at all costs if you want to leave significant value in the business. Frequently, business sales include a requirement for the business leader to contract to remain with the business for some time, often years after the sale was made.

 Planning is the key to exiting the business. When you formed or joined your business, did you expect to stay until you retired, leave in two to five years, or leave when the business had reached a stage or waypoint on its journey, achieving growth or profit of a particular level? Did you give any thought to when or how you might leave?

Knowing what you intend to do allows you to create an action plan and set targets to achieve. Having a good business model and business blueprint should enable you to systemize your business and make it less and less dependent upon you. Good businesses should appear to  run themselves and should be capable of being run by the same standards and in the same way, even if all the staff were to leave at one time.

BUSINESS OWNER EXIT

Consider the following matrix of factors:

1. Share liquidity (ease of sale)
2. Business performance (profit history)
3. Business potential
4. Asset value
5. Cash value

Professional investors such as venture capitalists and business angels plan their exits before they invest.

BUSINESS LEGACY

When your business is gone, what lasting legacy do you think it will leave? Is it important to leave a legacy? These are questions for you to answer. I personally think it would be good to think that the business could have a made a difference to the world in some small way.

I would hope that it would have provided lasting wealth to its shareholders and employees and that it has faithfully and diligently served its customers, enabling them to receive the outcomes they desired.

I happen to believe in a higher purpose than just the greed that lies at the heart of the business world. I believe the business reflects the contributions of its leaders and, as a business leader, I see the business as a small part of me. I want my values to be reflected in my business, and I also would like to think that those values could inspire others.

REAL-LIFE STORY

Barney Green was someone who had worked hard and done well, rising to the board of a construction industry business. He had been involved in a management buyout, but had ended up with a small minority stake. A civil engineer by trade, Barney had become a successful businessman.

Over time he grew frustrated by his position, where he lacked influence in terms of the business strategy. The other directors didn't seem to have an equity exit strategy in mind or even a coherent business plan. He saw his own successful division continually subsidizing or outperforming other divisions.

Barney didn't see his ambitions and dreams being realized within that company. He was someone with a fairly clear idea about what he wanted:

- Quality of life
- Financial security and stability
- Personal control of his own destiny
- The ability and wherewithal to buy or build a yacht and spend time sailing with his family

Seeing an opportunity in the niche field of construction industry safety, Barney grasped it with both hands. Barney was slightly apprehensive over giving up a regular salary and moving into the unknown. Not only was he forming a new company, but also he was creating a new market that didn't previously exist. This surely has to be one of the riskiest and most challenging things to do.

He took his major supplier into his new venture with a minority stake, which guaranteed his supply of materials and also financial and business support. As with all successful businesses, Barney took on a huge amount of hard work. He overcame challenge after challenge such as inertia, market acceptance, and the ability to generate increasing revenues. Success brought rewards, both financial and personal. He felt the exhilaration of seeing his creation flourish, creating opportunities for others, and having his efforts recognized.

What was, perhaps, less motivating was when others saw his success and decided to compete, compromising market prices and work standards. Just when he was doing well he encountered the inevitable setbacks. How he picked himself up and dealt with those setbacks was what set him apart. Business can be tough and Barney experienced setbacks that could have made less determined people give up. First was a spate of bad debts, followed by the failure of his insurance company, and then a five-fold increase in insurance premiums. Despite all this he stuck to his vision, responded to changing circumstances, and looked for a suitable buyer to fulfill his exit strategy. He achieved this by selling his business, but even this was not without its difficulties. The new inexperienced owner managed to destroy the business before he had even finished paying for it.

For Barney, one adventure was over and new ones were underway already. He had his yacht ready for his family voyage and a new business taking root too. Among all this excitement, however, Barney's family suffered the loss of their ten-year-old daughter, who died suddenly of a brain hemorrhage. Life and business are both adventures full of risk and uncertainty. We should never forget that time is our most precious asset and we must learn to cherish it and make the most of it; none of us knows how much of it we have left.

Lessons to learn
- ❑ Recognize when you are dissatisfied with your current situation.
- ❑ Think of a new idea and have the motivation to do something about it.
- ❑ Set yourself clear objectives.
- ❑ Select suitable partners to share the adventure.
- ❑ Be prepared to overcome hellish challenges.
- ❑ Focus on executing your plan.

Engineers would never dream of trying to build a fine machine from any old parts or materials they could find. They would design and specify materials, tolerances, measurements, and accurate plans. Your business, too, needs thought and design, process and controls, measurements and instruments. Your business, among other things, is a legal, money-making machine. Make sure it works and reap the rewards!

CHAPTER 8:

The Business Blueprint

Business Blueprint Introduction

In the previous chapters we looked at the challenges facing business leaders in conceiving, setting up, and running their businesses. Arguably, being in business has never been so difficult, but at the same time the opportunities may never have been greater. One of the wonderful things about business is that it is possible to achieve great things from very humble beginnings and sometimes all within a very short timeframe. There has never been more advice available; the sources of information and knowledge have never been richer. Go into any major library and you can find an overwhelming range of books on every business topic you can possibly imagine. For each of these books, hundreds and possibly thousands of man-hours of effort have gone into research, writing, and producing them. Today there are seminars on everything under the sun, training courses on subjects you'd never been previously aware of, and yet achieving success seems just as difficult as ever.

Some businesses become successful by chance and are successful despite their business leaders not because of them. If one accepts that business leaders are in charge, the question begs what do they need to do to find the success they desire? In many cases business leaders will score ten out of ten for effort, but the only thing that matters is achievement and sometimes that can be an elusive dream.

Many different factors come together to affect the success of the business. It is always difficult to establish which of the factors is the most important.

The business world is chaotic and fast-moving. It is very difficult to see the big picture, the business as a whole. When you are deep within the business, it is very difficult to see yourself as others see you. In the preceding chapters,

we looked at many of the issues you have to face and looked at some key concepts. To move forward, you need to create a business blueprint that makes sense of the chaotic and confused business world and puts order and predictability into your business. As a business leader, you might feel you are holding lots of balls and continually juggling them until the point a new ball arrives and you start to drop them.

One of the key secrets of your business success is creating a business blueprint. The business blueprint is more closely related to you, the business leader, than you might initially think. Business leaders hold the keys to success but find it difficult to unlock the success they desire. The word "hold" is particularly relevant, because in the majority of businesses the problem lies with the fact that the business leaders hold the business in their minds. The business needs them to function; they are continually making decisions, directing people, and getting involved in the day-to-day activities of business.

The basic principle of the business blueprint is to transfer the weight of the business from the burdened shoulders of its leaders to the business's own systems. The idea is that the system runs the business and the business leaders run the system. The system is documented and enshrined in operational and procedural guidebooks, which rather than gather dust on the shelves, are used by each and every person involved in the business. Not surprisingly this is linked to quality, which can be defined as a "grade of excellence," an "accomplishment" or "attainment." Your business is trying to achieve shareholder value predominantly by making profits.

 An easier way to visualize this is to first consider your business as an entity in its own right that can exist and function even if you are not involved at all and second, to consider your business itself as a giant machine which makes profit, the "profit-making machine." Can you see how attractive it would be to go into work every morning, turn on your machine and sit back and watch the profit fall out of the end of the machine and into your bank account? Can you see the difference between being in the business of selling widgets and being in the business of running a profit-making machine? Your profit-making machine might make and sell widgets as part of what it does to make profit, but it is only part of what it does. Your profit-making machine does more than make and sell its products. It carries out a complex range of activities to add value to your business, it drives operational efficiency, reduces costs, creates brand value, develops customer relationships, designs new products and services, and marketing programs that enable you to cross sell, up sell, etc.

You might well be reading this thinking I do those things anyway. The difference I am trying to portray is that your profit-making machine links together all these things you do or perhaps should be doing, and binds them together to work as a whole.

Imagine each of the things you do as a cog. You have a marketing cog whose purpose is to position your business and create sales opportunities; this cog is linked to your sales cog whose purpose is to deliver profitable sales. Your sales cog is linked to your administration cog whose purpose is to manage your relationships with customers, suppliers, potential customers, and service and support them and the business. Your administration and sales cogs are linked to your accounting and finance cog whose purpose is to ensure that your customers have enough money to pay you, you have enough funds to support the requirements of the business, and that you pay your taxes and comply with the legal restrictions placed upon you by law. You then have your operations cog that manufactures your products. Your distribution cog distributes your products to your customers. This has to be linked to your accounting and administration cogs so they know your customer has received the goods and is due to pay you and back to the sales cog so the salesman knows if you have fulfilled your delivery promise. There are, of course, many more cogs.

Imagine now that all these cogs are linked together and somewhere there is a big handle that, when you turn it, all the cogs move together with perfect ratios between them. This is your profit-making machine. Now think about what is possibly happening in your business. You still have these same cogs, but they are not linked together in a structured format. They are possibly linked together in your mind and the minds of some of your colleagues — it's common sense. I think most people would agree, however, that in this scenario you are holding all the balls, and it's just a matter of time before you start to drop them.

In the profit-making machine model, the machine itself holds the balls and there is no chance that they will be dropped. The machine carries the burden; the machine does the work. This frees you up to improve the machine to make yet more profit. An ideal, but when you look at the world's most successful organizations, they create highly-tuned, effective profit-making machines.

We looked earlier at the wonder of military organizations and how they perhaps represented a role model to follow. If you look under the surface, you will see they are one big machine whose purpose may not be to generate profit, but to deliver the outcomes desired by its most senior leaders, the government. Whether you ask military machines to fight terrorism, bring down corrupt regimes, or step in to manage crises or disasters anywhere, the military machines make it happen, seemingly with total ease.

The plans and designs of your own profit-making machine comprise your business blueprint. The difference between using a profit-making machine and not is predictability and consistency of results. It is, of course, possible to be highly successful without using a profit-making machine. But you will work harder and you will find it very difficult to be consistent on a day-to-day basis, unless your staff is highly committed, been in their jobs a long time, and nothing out of the ordinary occurs. The difference can be likened to doing manual work or to automating the work by installing a machine. The Industrial Revolution has taught us that manufacturing efficiency can best be guaranteed by the use of better and better machines. Why not, therefore, consider the business as a whole to be a machine?

KEY BUSINESS FACTS

There are some facts that you need to know about your business. The key players involved in your business are you, the business leader, your employees, customers, shareholders, and suppliers. Each of these different participants wants to get different things out of the business; they all have their own legitimate perspectives. You need to understand them and appreciate what they mean. Ignore the interests of these participants at your peril.

Everyone needs to know

- This is who we are.
- This is what we do.

Customer perspective

- This is how we do it.
- This is what you can expect from us.
- This is why you should use us.

Employee perspective

- What is expected of me?
- What do I have to do?
- What's in it for me?

Shareholder perspective

- What is the value proposition?
- Why should I invest in the business?
- What is my likely return on investment?
- When am I likely to receive it?

COMMON MISTAKES

In ninety-nine percent of cases, when new businesses are formed the business and the business leaders are indistinguishable. Everything is in the head of the business leaders: the business purpose, the product service offerings, positioning, strategies, ideas, etc.

The business simply could not exist without the business leader. They are the people who know everything that is going on. They are in control; they know what they are doing and initially at least they are probably enjoying being center stage. Nothing is more rewarding than to arrive at a new prospective customer and hand over your business card, which proudly states under your name that you are the proprietor, managing director, chairman, and chief executive officer.

You are the boss, you walk tall, you are the person who makes the decisions, and your status in the business world has increased tenfold. Everyone likes to deal with the boss, the decision maker, and the person who runs the show. I can assure you there are times when this situation makes you feel very good about yourself. Over time you will realize that it has some major drawbacks such as those that plague inexperienced business leaders. They are easy to recognize by these telltale signs:

- Their mobile phones are virtually stuck to their ears.
- They are always in a rush.
- They never have enough time to do all the things they need to do.
- They are always at the center of activities.
- They have always got their fingers in other people's business.
- They work long hours.

- There are always lots of messages for them; they constantly have to get back to people.
- They are continually multi-tasking, doing the work, the administration, the accounts, etc.
- They are always slightly behind their busy schedule.
- They are constantly harassed.

As a business leader you will find that, over time, you become the target of other company's sales people. They want to speak to you and only you; they will pamper your ego, make you feel good about yourself; respect you for being the boss. The downside is, however, that they are after your money and they, metaphorically speaking, are trying to get their sticky fingers into your wallet and your bank account. You have become a target for salesmen, they distract you, they demand your time, and they prevent you from concentrating on running your business.

You do, of course, need quality suppliers and business partners. You need their time and if you are wise, you realize you can get these people to add lots of value to your business for no charge whatsoever. Salesmen from other companies will tell you what your competitors are doing, what is happening in the market, and they will be sources of free business advice.

IS THERE A BETTER WAY?

Common mistakes have been defined above, but maybe they are not mistakes at all. Isn't this just business life? Isn't this what everyone goes through and experiences at some time or another? Isn't it perfectly normal?

The answers to all these questions are obviously down to personal opinion. I would suggest that experienced and inexperienced business leaders would accept that some of the situations I have defined are broadly true or at least have elements of truth.

The key question is, "Is there a better way?" How could things be better for both the business and the business leader? Could it be possible to create a situation where:

- The business runs like clockwork as precisely as the atomic clock?
- The business leaders focus their efforts not on running the business but making the business better and more successful?
- The business runs on a day–to-day basis with little or no involvement from the business leader?
- Customers know exactly what the business stands for and what they can expect from it?
- There is total consistency on a day-to-day basis?
- Everyone working within the business understands the purpose and objectives of the business and how their work contributes to the success of the business?
- The business becomes orderly and not chaotic?
- Every aspect of the business runs quietly, efficiently, quickly, and cost effectively?
- No event makes the business wobble because every eventuality has been thought through?
- When something does go wrong, it is dealt with so swiftly, professionally, and efficiently you are left marveling at how this was achieved?
- There are virtually no surprises?
- The business delivers profits month after month, year after year?
- The business leader's quality of life is exceptional?
- The business leaders achieve the exact rewards that they set out to achieve?
- Business growth is limited purely to the desires of the business leaders?

You might be thinking that the above represents a totally unrealistic and unachievable ideal. Surely this just isn't possible, and life cannot be that good, can it? Wouldn't it be good, in fact wouldn't it be brilliant, if you could achieve the above? If I were to tell you this was possible and you could have it all, would that be something of interest to you?

What would it be worth to you if I revealed the secrets that would enable you to achieve just this? Surely what we are talking about here is the golden touch, the alchemy, the magical power or process of transmuting things of low value to high value, a universal solvent, and an elixir of life, something that is too good to be true.

Would you believe it if you saw it? You probably would, we all need proof to enable us to accept the improbable. The proof is all around you, you just have to look for it.

STOP! ARE YOU READY FOR THE JOURNEY TO ENLIGHTENMENT?

Have I got your attention? Are you now ready to start this short journey to enlightenment? If you are not, you should not proceed beyond this point.

If you want to understand how you can achieve these things yourself, I can show you the route to take. Before I do, I need to ask you some basic questions. Your answers to these questions will determine whether you will be able to understand the concepts I am about to reveal to you.

There are three steps I am going to take you through. If you understand them, I promise you that your business and your private lives are very likely to never be the same again. I must warn you that this is a one-way process. You will never mentally be able to go back once you have made these discoveries. Once you know, you will know, like discovering the truth about Father Christmas and tooth fairies.

If you are able to pass the following induction test, you will be able to join an exclusive club of business leaders.

Step 1

❑ Do you believe in logic and reason? (These are supported by knowledge and experience.)

❑ Do you believe in cause and effect? (Everything you do has a result, good, bad, or neutral.)

❑ Do you believe you can influence your own life and your own business?

❑ To pass Step 1, you need to have answered yes to all three questions.

❑ If you did not, I strongly suggest you should not be in business and if you are, your business will be destined for eventual failure.

Step 2

Having passed Step 1, you now need to answer the following questions:

❑ Do you believe it is possible to use logic and reason and cause and effect to define choices and actions in your business and private life?

❑ If the answer to the above question is yes, can you accept that your choices and actions influence your business and private life?

❑ If you can answer yes to both questions, proceed to Step 3. If you answered no to one or both, question why you are in business.

Step 3

❑ Do you believe that motivation is needed to make choices and take actions?

❑ If the answer to this question is yes, you have passed the induction.

Enlightenment

In passing the induction test, you have proved you understand:

- You have the ability to make choices and instigate actions.

- Your choices and actions will deliver outcomes/results.

- You can influence the outcomes and results by applying reason and logic to the choices you make, supported by knowledge and experience.

- You have the implements of control, but you need motivation to use them.

Logic and reason are linked to choices, and cause and effect is linked to actions.

Actions (doing something) create causes (things happening) that have effects, which in turn deliver outcomes (the result of what has happened).

Personal mantra

I am in control of my life and business.

I have the ability to determine the outcomes I desire.

Skeptics might be seriously unimpressed by the above. It is, after all, just common sense. Why is it, therefore, that despite business leaders being in control of their own lives and businesses, so many are not achieving the outcomes they desire in either?

This is the question that needs answering, but to do so, you need to understand the principles above. Could it be that we often are too busy with the hustle and bustle of daily life and the immediate issues that we don't think about the long-term outcomes we desire? Could it also be that our motivation is insufficient? If we wanted to achieve the longer-term outcomes we claim we desire, why do we lose track of them? To be honest, are the decisions and choices we make on a day-to-day basis made with conscious thought about how they are going to help us achieve those longer-term goals? Do you think that may explain why so many of us fail to achieve them?

 Let's go back and consider the things that we were looking to achieve. For example:

- The business runs like clockwork as precisely as the atomic clock.

- The business leaders focus their efforts not on running the business, but making the business better and more successful.

- The business runs on a day-to-day basis with little or no involvement from the business leader.

What would it take for our business to run like clockwork, as precisely as an atomic clock? First, we get to apply logic and reason. This might be that for the business to run like clockwork it needs to have predictability, it needs to be foolproof, reliable, and accurate.

We then need to ask the question, how can we create an organization that is predictable, foolproof, reliable, and accurate? We might decide that the way to do this is to think of our business as a machine, because good machines are predictable, foolproof, reliable, and accurate. A good machine will run all day long, creating identical copies of the same product. In fact, it will continue to run until it either breaks down or somebody turns it off.

We might continue to use logic and reason to develop the concept further by looking at all the component parts and identifying what they would have to do and what they would look like. The result is that you eventually make a choice to build a machine. Your actions are to actually build it. The effect of your actions is that you have a machine. You then turn the machine on and see if it works, has it delivered the outcomes you expected, does your business now run like clockwork? If it does, that is fantastic. If it doesn't, you can use logic and reason to understand why it doesn't. You can then make choices to take actions to improve or change your machine so it does work.

As a business leader, your primary role should be to build your business machine and work continually on improving it. The business machine must be visible to everyone involved in the business — employees, customers, suppliers, advisors, etc. Invisible machines that can be seen only by you are useless. The aim is to make you and your business two completely different things. Your business is not you and you are not your business. This might sound obvious, but many businesses struggle to survive without continual input from the business leaders.

What is going to make your business machine visible? Imagine that rather than creating your business machine just for you, you are, in fact, creating a business machine that is going to be used by tens of thousands of people from all over the world, from every country, background, and every walk of life. Any inefficiency in any part of the machine is going to be replicated ten thousand times. Imagine the impact this might have operationally and financially, imagine the cost of putting it right. In this scenario you have to think very carefully about the reasons and logics for making choices and also the cause and effect of actions. It is fundamentally important to understand the role of your business machine, what you are trying to achieve with your business, what business you are looking to be in, how much profit you want to make, and by when. Do you want a machine that makes a $1000, $10,000, $100,000, or $1 million a week? Are you looking to create a Lamborghini or a Yugo?

With 10,000 business machines all over the world, you have no idea who is going to be using them. You have to assume that the users are from different walks of life and this machine has to be designed for ordinary, not extraordinary people. Imagine the problems you would have if 10,000 people called you up and asked you for help using the machine. You simply could not cope.

What you have to do is deliberate carefully about the purpose of your machine. For example, who is going to use it, why they are going to use it, when they are going to use it, and where they are going to use it? There could be few or many potential variations. Imagine dispatching these business machines from your factory and sending them out to the 10,000 locations, making sure that within the box is every single component they need to make that machine work, including user guides, maintenance instructions, enhancement tool kits, breakdown instructions, etc.

What would these boxes contain and what would they look like? How could you portray these? The answer lies in your business blueprint.

BUILDING YOUR BUSINESS BLUEPRINT — PROFIT-MAKING MACHINE

If your business can be likened to a machine, the blueprint represents the engineers' and designers' drawings and plans. The designer will always produce drawings from a variety of different perspectives to enable the viewers to properly visualize them.

Visualization

To create your business blueprint you need to be able to visualize your business as you intend it to be in the future. The visualization should be a part of the business conception process. A good analogy can be made between large-scale building developments. The designers and architects produce a range of drawings in plan view, but also with elevations. It is also common to produce physical, three-dimensional models that are made to scale. Where the investments are large, three-dimensional computer modeling is sometimes used to enable those who are interested to experience the building before it is built. By creating this visualization, it is possible to see whether the building will work. What does it look like when the sun shines through the windows? Is it practical or aesthetically pleasing? What does it look like with a thousand people inside?

You might want to consider visualizing the following aspects of your business:

- ❑ The industry you are in
- ❑ Products and services that you are likely to be selling
- ❑ Who your customers are going to be
- ❑ How many customers you are going to have
- ❑ Where you are going to be located
- ❑ How you are going to market and sell your products and services
- ❑ How you are going to source and deliver your products and services
- ❑ How you are going to administer the business
- ❑ Who is going to do the work
- ❑ What the organization will look like
- ❑ How the business will be controlled and managed
- ❑ What results you expect the business to achieve (profitability/shareholder growth)

The business visualization is intended to give a high-level picture of the business as if you are looking at it from a distance. It is the equivalent of the "artist's impression," not the engineer's drawings. The cost and effort of changing the drawings or designs before the building is built can be many hundreds of thousands of times less than trying to make the changes after the building has been built.

The same issues are present in the design of businesses. Anyone with experience of large, corporate business-system implementations will also be aware that it is better to spend extra time planning and ensuring that the system specifications are right before they undertake any development work. As often happens, failings of the system are only realized when the system is about to be implemented and the users review it or, worse still, after it has actually been implemented.

Because the only constant in business is continual change, this factor needs to be built into your business design. Furthermore, when designing any aspect of your business take into account the possible economic life of each aspect.

In summary, it is very important to visualize what your business will be like in the future. You may need to consider a large number of different scenarios. If your business blueprint could be likened to a painting, you start with a blank canvas and frame, roughly sketch the key components of the picture, and then slowly, painstakingly, complete the detail.

Building blocks

Creating a good business blueprint that is going to work is a very difficult task. If it were easy and straightforward, everyone would do it. If you use the painting-by-numbers analogy, the building blocks that follow

represent the canvas and outline on which the picture is created. You need the outline and the frame before you can create a meaningful picture. These building blocks represent the foundations and provide structure to what can be confusing issues.

Once you have identified these basic building blocks, the real work of putting in the detail begins. For example, one of the company's objectives might be to make one million dollars profit this year. The impact of this might be the sales department needs an objective to sell ten million dollars worth of products and services. The manufacturing department might have the objective to make ten million dollars worth of products. The sales department might have a number of different divisions that all need their own objectives, which dovetail into the overall objective. This linkage between different aspects of the business is the process that enables the creation of the entire business profit-making machine.

Develop a company vision

When business leaders establish and run businesses, they need to know what it is they want to achieve and have some idea of how they are going to achieve it, what they are going to do, what they are going to manufacture, sell, deliver, etc. The vision represents the future, their dream about the business and what it is going to do.

The vision represents a destination or at least a waypoint on a long route. In some ways the starting point is the end point. The vision defines what you would like to achieve in the broadest terms, which enables you to lay plans for what you need to do to achieve it.

Develop a company mission

The mission is what the business is going to do to achieve the vision. Missions tend to look to the shorter term and provide the incremental steps to achieve the vision.

Define the company's goals and objectives

The vision represents the highest levels of goals and objectives. This can be too generic and imprecise to be of much use by itself.

Goals and objectives need to be set for every part and aspect of the business and should dovetail into one another. If these objectives and goals are continually met, the vision will be achieved.

Create your strategy

Strategy represents the high level of "how to." It defines the methods by which the goals and objectives will be achieved. There are many ways to achieve objectives. The best strategy will achieve the best result most quickly and efficiently.

Create company policies

Policies define a course or line of action to be adopted and pursued within the business. They are the rules.

Policies may define benefits, identify performance measures and organizational levels, define organizational constraints, and identify workflows and processes.

Create procedures and processes

Procedures define the way in which actions are conducted. They ensure consistency, no matter who is performing the action.

Create organizational structure

The organizational structure defines the organization's locations, work groups, and reporting structure. It enables command and control through the use of hierarchies and authorizations.

Determine roles

Roles represent a part of the organizational hierarchy, which is attributable to a particular job function. A manager, for example, might be allocated the role of health and safety coordinator in addition to his other duties and other roles. The role represents the area or function that needs to be addressed within the business.

DEFINITIONS

Roles need to be clearly defined with terms of reference so the people fulfilling them know what their duties and responsibilities are.

Identification of positions/job descriptions

People have jobs and are employed in positions within the business, e.g., salesmen, accountants, customer service representatives, etc. An individual might be employed for a particular position and that position might require them to fulfill different roles. An example might be a salesman whose primary role is to sell, has a secondary role as customer relationship manager, and a third role as accounts receivable representative responsible for collecting late payments.

Experience profiles

To fill a position, individuals need to have enough experience to enable them to do the things that will be asked of them. Levels of experience required will vary.

Competencies

Competencies are the skills needed to carry out the jobs. Well-defined competencies make it easier to screen for qualified candidates.

Qualifications

Qualifications are the circumstances or conditions required to perform job duties. For example, to be a delivery driver, you need to have a valid driver's license.

Performance measures

The business can achieve its objectives only if those people working in it contribute positively. To determine whether they are contributing positively, establish performance measures, then measure their performance against them.

Identification of tasks

A position can only be effectively fulfilled if the roles allocated to the position are correctly fulfilled. People fulfill these roles by completing activities (tasks).

BUILDING COGS

The building blocks provide the structure; the "Cogs" represent departmental or functional areas:

- Departmental areas: Marketing, Sales, Operations, etc.

- Functional areas: Leadership, Measurement, Analysis, etc.

Each departmental area has its own departmental vision, mission, objectives, strategies, policies and procedures, organization, tasks, roles, and positions. The functional cogs support the departmental cogs.

Examples of Departmental Cogs

- Marketing

- Sales

- Manufacturing

- Purchasing

- Operations/Delivery

- Administration and Support

- Finance and Accounting

- Credit and Risk Management

Examples of Functional Cogs

- Leadership

- Control

- Legal Compliance

- Health and Safety

- Quality

- Infrastructure

Ranking cogs by importance

While the business arguably needs all the cogs and is only as good as its weakest link, some are clearly more important (mission-critical) than others. For example, with no sales function/department, your business isn't likely to sell anything. Most businesses need to sell to stay in business. However you could probably survive without your employee massage department. Think of the radio breaking in your car: it doesn't stop your driving the car, but it does prevent one form of entertainment from enhancing your travel experience.

 It is very important to grade your cogs, establishing which cogs are mission-critical, which are important, and which are nice to have. Logically, you should focus your attention on these according to their importance. You must always ask the question, "What would be the consequence of this cog not working at all or working poorly?"

Assembling and integrating cogs

Each cog on its own is useless. Only when it is connected to others can worthwhile outcomes be created. The sequence of cogs represents the processes deployed within the business. For example, marketing activities normally precede sales activities; they create leads and opportunities that can be converted into sales. A sale will mean that a delivery will need to be fulfilled, an invoice created and payment received.

The assembling of cogs can be likened to "Business Process Re-Engineering," a business concept that was popular in the 1990s and which fuelled the meteoric rise of. ERP-integrated business computer application systems such as SAP.

Turning the handle

Imagine if marketing was the first cog in your profit-making machine. The marketing cog creates sales opportunities. If turning the handle means making marketing work and the output is sales opportunities, then the marketing cog will be working properly and will link with the sales cog. This picks up the sales opportunities and converts them to firm sales orders. The sales cog is working and then links to the operations cog. If marketing doesn't work and create any leads, then sales have no opportunities to work on and the machine won't work.

The faster the marketing handle is turned the greater the number of sales opportunities and so on.

Machine controls

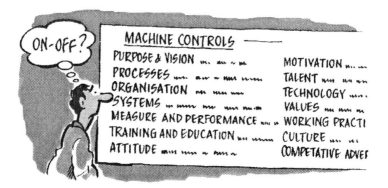

For the machine to work, it needs controls, which enable settings to be implemented. It also needs gauges, which monitor the performance of the machine. Controls and gauges might be as follows:

- Purpose and vision
- Processes
- Organization

- Systems
- Measures and performance
- Training and education
- Attitude
- Motivation
- Talent
- Technology
- Values
- Working practices
- Culture
- Competitive advantage benchmarking

BUSINESS BLUEPRINT STEP BY STEP

The starting point of your business blueprint should be the end point or a waypoint on your planned voyage. You will think and brainstorm first.

 Answer the following questions:

1. What am I looking to achieve and by when?

2. What would need to happen to enable that to be achieved?

3. What are the most critical actions and achievements needed?

Step 1 Create and communicate your building blocks starting with documenting your vision.

Step 2 Identify the cogs you need and document them.

Step 3 Assemble your cogs and decide how they link together and interface.

Step 4 Decide what controls and measurements you need and document them.

Step 5 Identify what resources you need to achieve your objectives:

- People
- Skills
- Money
- Equipment
- Resources
- Infrastructure

Employees (People)

- ❑ Selection
- ❑ Induction
- ❑ Training
- ❑ Employee Management
- ❑ Measurement Analysis
- ❑ Control
- ❑ Direction
- ❑ Reward
- ❑ Recognition
- ❑ Discipline
- ❑ Motivation
- ❑ Attitude

Tasks (Actions)

- ❏ Identification
- ❏ Function
- ❏ Reason
- ❏ Responsibility
- ❏ Accountability
- ❏ Objective
- ❏ Performance Measure
- ❏ Process
- ❏ Quality
- ❏ Controls
- ❏ Interfaces/Impacts

REAL-LIFE STORY

I have been involved with many different businesses and have had many business adventures, but the first business I floated is one that stands out as a beacon and deserves some attention.

An adventure can be described as "an undertaking involving risk and uncertainty in the hope of positive outcomes with the expectation of excitement." This story begins with a clear vision of an exciting positive outcome to grow a business from roughly $750,000 turnover to $36 million in three years. In today's market this seems unlikely, but in the midst of the technology sector boom this sort of enormous growth was highly possible, given the right business conditions and sufficient resources.

The business conception happened as a result of my idea, and my motivation to do something about it. I created a story, which any business plan is, that was logical and made sense to the average person. This story was backed up by independent evidence to support it. For example, Steve Ballmer, President of Microsoft, went on record as saying that the application category I was intending to enter "was likely to be the hottest application category for the next five years."

Investors are driven by greed and fear. At the time the market was bullish; investors appeared to be winning more than losing as the financial markets continued to rise. The dot-com boom was at its height, and confidence was high.

Being an author, I have some aptitude for creating stories. I understand that words are powerful and can make or lose fortunes and change lives. I realized that good stories need to be honed and improved, and this is  just what I set about doing. I sought assistance from others, making the story better and better. No man or women is an island; we can rarely achieve great things on our own. I was no exception.

As I look back, I can see that I practiced many of the habits Stephen Covey reveals in his book, *7 Habits of Highly Effective People*:

- Be proactive.
- Begin with the end in mind.
- Put first things first.
- Think win/win.
- Seek first to understand then be understood.
- Synergize.
- Sharpen the saw.

I started by being proactive, writing the story on paper and learning to verbally articulate it. The story supported the objective (the end result). Using the power of the story, I started to recruit a team of people who were interested in the end result and what it could mean to them. I have learned that when you have a good story, high caliber people are often very keen to follow. Having good people makes the story stronger. I learned that by putting first things first, I was able to build steps that could take me closer to my goal.

Knowing who you are and what you want is difficult, but if you can work out who you are and what you want, it is easier to successfully achieve your goal. Being someone whose goals are big and ambitious meant that I was able to create an inspiring vision. The world actually needs people to go out and innovate and create opportunities for others. I recognized that the achievement of my dream would enable the dreams of others to be realized too. What can be more inspiring than helping others to achieve their dreams? Dreams create belief and positive energy that can further help fuel success.

When I first approached city advisors, I realized that for all their strengths and experience, the fundraising is possible only through the efforts of entrepreneurs like me who have the courage to stand up and be counted and who believe in their ideas and are motivated to do something about them. There is the danger that a humble entrepreneur can seek too much approval and too much guidance from advisors and won't be successful. At the end of the day, it is your idea, your business, and your journey you are selling. Advisors will do their best to impart their knowledge and experience, but we live in a fast-changing world where innovation alters the future and the past is not always the best predictor of the future. Advisers are looking for entrepreneurs who can demonstrate leadership, who know what they want, and how they intend to get it. Leadership is important from the very beginning.

I realized my vision was equally valid within a large range of scales. A business could have been created with $500, $5000, $50,000, $500,000, $5 million, or $50 million. It all comes down to the story. I chose a story that needed approximately $10 million. Another story could have been created for a different amount. I chose a market to list on and set about achieving my first ever initial placement offer (IPO). At the time, approximately $10 million would be the biggest amount ever achieved by an IPO on the small market I chose. I also decided I wanted to list within three months.

There were many who said that it was impossible to raise such a large sum or to do it so quickly, but with my new team I proved them wrong on both counts. As it was, we raised nearly $12 million and had to hand back almost $2 million. I left nothing to chance; I was involved in everything, and I personally made sure I sold our story to as many people as possible. I went on television and had articles written about us in national newspapers.

Overnight, I was personally worth approximately $38 million, owned eighty percent of a company with close to $10 million in the bank, and was on a generous employment contract.

(*Note: The values mentioned are approximate and are based on an exchange rate USD/GBP which will vary over time.*)

I wrote my vision, a sixteen-page document that covered the following:

- What are our reasons for being in business?
- What business are we in?
- What size do we want to be over a given time frame?
- How ambitious are we?
- What is our company culture?
- What are our values?
- What are our beliefs?
- How should we be benchmarked against other organizations?
- What position do we want to be in our market?
- What markets do we want to be in?
- What do we think our business life cycle will be?
- What things are most important to us?

Being a technology-related service business, the greatest perceived risk in our business plan was that we wouldn't be able to recruit and train enough people. Through meticulous planning and some innovation, we managed to achieve what others thought was impossible. The business setup and the business model development seemed to be going well, while we built up to an employee base of nearly a hundred. As we embarked upon our business voyage, we were full of hope and enthusiasm.

When people joined we asked them why and some of the first responses were as follows:

Employee 1

I joined Jonathan because of his beliefs, he knew where he was going and he was selling tickets for the ride. I bought a ticket; it's as simple as that.

I am lucky enough to have been part of the company from the beginning — two guys in a garage in the middle of winter is not fun, I can assure you. It has been one hell of a ride, going from virtually nothing for a year to this growing, thriving organization that we are all a part of now. The one thing that to me has stayed the same are the company's values of honesty and integrity. These are a very important part of the company and have helped it to what it is today and what it will be in the future.

Employee 2

Having just worked for a large corporation, I found the formal and regimental atmosphere claustrophobic and indifferent and was really seeking something to challenge me. I met with Jonathan and within a half hour he had me writing out my own offer letter. I found his approach totally different to any other I had experienced and his energy and drive left me feeling really excited about working for him and the company. I have always been very keen to work for a company from the start and really feel that my contributions mattered, where their values included looking after their people (customers and staff), where they do what they say they are going to do, and where they ensure that although you work hard you also have fun at the same time. I realized all these desires in this company.

Employee 3

I wanted to be part of a new company that promoted my own values, encouraged and developed my skills, and wanted me to have fun while working!

Employee 4

I joined because I enjoy the challenge of taking up the opportunity of being involved in a new company and helping to build a successful team while enjoying myself at the same time.

Employee 5

After hearing about the company values of working hard and maintaining high customer care standards, as well as having fun while you work, I was swept up in the excitement of this new company ideal.

Employee 6

I joined because I found their vision, ethos, and business strategies to be exciting and refreshing. The variety of job functions and career path scope offered was excellent. I was also very keen to be part of a new company and play my role in their successful growth, right from the beginning.

What happened next shocked every single employee and investor. Quite simply the market did not materialize as everyone had expected, and we were not able to generate the sales we anticipated. At first the analysts predicted the market was just slow to take off but would still happen. The Y2K computer issue was blamed for stopping new investment in technology. Slowly the technology market started to crumble, and some giants were reduced to dust. The freefall had started and so, too, had the dot-com and technology financial market crash. The float was in March and by September the share price had started to tumble as did the bank balance. We had little choice but to release most of the new employees who had joined with such excitement.

As livelihoods were at stake, the pressure was immense. Everyone wanted to search for someone to blame. The strong team spirit that was created turned against the business. We acquired our biggest competitor — with nearly twenty employees and a large customer base — out of receivership. The reasoning for doing this was sound, but in reality it caused a clash of cultures and values and resulted in much resentment.

Just one year later the powerful story was gone and new stories needed to be created based on the present realities. We recruited someone we believed to be a high-caliber, experienced, and expensive sales director and made the decision to move into a different but related business sector that was doing well. As we did this, that market sector collapsed too.

I have never so acutely realized the danger of overdependence on any one individual. The new sales director forecast future sales on which the company based future decisions. Slowly, but surely, the forecasts failed to materialize. We then discovered the sales director was an instigator of a conspiracy to set up a competing business with some of our other employees. Corporate skullduggery at its worst!

Being in a business when things are going wrong is like being in the thick of a military battle — there is confusion everywhere and it is difficult to tell who is friend or foe and who might defect at any time. The pressures on everyone, especially me, were immense. I wished to be almost anywhere other than where I was. It was like being in a storm at sea.

Time became our most precious asset, and we had to make sure we'd survive long enough to let conditions improve. The sales director, for example, needed to be given time to generate sales, but equally, it took time to dismiss him on discovery of his dishonesty and malice. We had to follow proper procedures, otherwise, the bad guys might win, which happened once.

To add insult to injury, I acquired a business. The owner turned out to be dishonest and malicious. We were fortunate enough to recover some of our losses in this respect from our insurance company.

From a personal perspective, I was focused on objectivity and finding the truth about everything, including my own weaknesses. As the captain of a ship that was in trouble, I had to accept responsibility, but needed to know the real cause of the trouble to be able to do something about it. In many cases it is not just one thing, but a combination of many things that result in the outcomes we receive.

To a pressured and disheartened crew, the captain is to blame. It is easy for everyone, including the captain, to abandon ship, but values and integrity are important to me. A business voyage is full of risk and uncertainty; you won't always achieve your goals. I believe we shouldn't cry over spilled milk. There is nothing we can change about the past. In my mind the true measure of a person is how he behaves in times of adversity. Look at most successful entrepreneurs, and you will find that not all of their businesses are successful.

I had never looked harder and deeper at myself than during this turbulent time. How could it be that one person thinks you are the best boss they have ever had and others think you are the worst? I have come to realize that reality is in the eye of the beholder. As human beings with unique minds and personalities, "we see the world, not as it is, but as we are," in other words, from our perspective. My friend, Barney Green, once said to me when talking about business leaders and entrepreneurs, his definition of intelligence is "being able to continually question yourself" and search for the different perspectives on the issues you are facing.

The story needs to be rewritten continually in light of the reality of the moment. Many questions arise over when or if to give up. As a director of a publicly quoted company, I have moral and fiduciary responsibility to act in the best interests of all our shareholders, but I additionally feel tremendous personal responsibility to all the people who invested. From an entrepreneur's perspective, there is a big difference between being accountable just to yourself or to others. You need to be able to operate as the entrepreneur, manager, and worker. Being a major shareholder and also chief executive of a publicly quoted company is a little strange. You can't treat the company as if it were your own, because you own only part of it. As a director, you have duties and responsibilities as an officer of the company, but you are an employee with rights and responsibilities too.

It is all too easy to focus on success stories, but for every success there are usually many failures along the way. My advice is to act with integrity, stick to your values, and look for the truth, questioning yourself more than anyone else. Remember that the seed of equal or greater success is within every failure. At the very least you should learn from your experience and be more prepared next time. I could write a novel from this experience. I saw the very best and the very worst of human nature.

If you carry on doing what you are currently doing, you are likely to receive the same or worse results. If you want to achieve the business success you deserve and achieve the personal fulfillment and happiness you seek, you must take the necessary actions. Nothing will change unless you change it – the choice is yours.

CHAPTER 9:
Next Steps

TAKING THE NEXT STEPS

Billions of dollars are spent every year on business improvement, products, and services. If you have been in business for any time, you will no doubt be on the mailing lists of many different companies that would like to sell you places in training courses, seminars, or workshops. Go into any bookstore or library and you will find hundreds of books on almost every conceivable area of business improvement. There are many books on the same subject but the demand is clearly there.

Most business leaders have an insatiable hunger for knowledge. At times it seems like the entire world of business is seeking answers to the problems and issues it faces. It is rare to meet a businessman who has completely closed his mind to new ideas. Of course, it does sometimes happen and quite often these people have found the success they were seeking. As we said earlier, it is for you to define what success means to you; there are no hard and fast rules, no rights and wrongs, just theories and opinions.

My shelves are filled with business books and tapes and videos, business magazines and journals, old training course manuals. Over the years I have attended a large number of training courses on a huge variety of different subjects. I am struck by how short-lived the effects of the training and knowledge gathering have been. Every now and again I will pick up a book and thumb through its pages and I will get some more ideas and inspiration to help me tackle the challenges that I face. I keep coming back to the question, why are these effects short-lived? How much do we retain? I cannot help but think it is not very much.

Imagine if we were to retain all the knowledge and the skills we have learned, that each new skill and knowledge was added to an ever-increasing pile that was not only stored within ourselves, but could be used on a daily basis. I believe much of what we learn is still somewhere inside our subconscious mind and that if we had a metaphorical index system, we could look it up and use it whenever we need it.

I think some of the problems lie in the fact that some of the things we have learned conflict with each other, others overlap, and some disguise others. I think order and structure is a real problem. I also think it can be likened to having a large box full of puzzle pieces, i.e., you pick one up, you cannot see what it is, and it does not add any value. Put a few pieces together, and you might be able to see a part clearly. Put a few parts together, and you might be able to see an area clearly. But it is only when you put them all together that you see the big picture. That is when you can extract the value. You might have a few parts or areas in place, but you are only as good as your weakest link. So what can we do about this situation?

APPLY REASON AND LOGIC

The solution lies in accepting the situation as it is and applying reason and logic to the problem. If you cannot assemble the pieces of the puzzle in your head, then lay them out in front of you and start to put them together. From your pieces you will begin to see parts, as you assemble parts you will begin to see areas, and as you link the areas you will be able to see the whole.

I am sure you are thinking this is all well and good but my head is not full of puzzle pieces, so how can I assemble the thoughts, knowledge, and skills I have into a format I can use, a format that adds phenomenal value to my business and private life? I believe the answer lies in creating a written framework.

Some of you might remember painting by numbers as a child. These are kits you can buy where you are provided with a canvas with the picture divided into numbered parts like a framework. You are also provided with a guidebook that tells you what color to paint each frame and, of course, a completed picture to demonstrate what you are trying to achieve. To paint a picture from a blank canvas is something very few people can do well. Painting by numbers is something almost anyone can do because the complex and skilled task has been split into hundreds or thousands of easy-to-manage steps, the results look fantastic, and anyone not aware that the painting was done by numbers could be forgiven for thinking the artist was a genius, not a novice.

 Your business and personal life picture is a dynamic picture. It is forever changing. Picture those new horizons and stages in your life and you will see that you are painting a picture of your journey. The pictures provide you with understanding that enables you to make new choices/decisions and take new actions based on the knowledge and circumstances.

There are three steps you need to undertake:

1. Understand yourself.
2. Make choices and decisions.
3. Act upon them.

Looking at the three lines above, it seems the easiest thing on earth. There are only three things to think about. The reality is the absolute opposite. If you rank positive change on a scale from one to one hundred and measure it against books or training courses you have attended, the likelihood is the positive change for books could well be between one and ten and between five and twenty for training courses. As time passes, these values decrease. Understanding is the easiest step. Making choices and decisions is the next easiest step to take. But taking actions and making them work is incredibly difficult, particularly where other people are involved. It is as if we are sieves, where so much of what we take in just comes straight out again. Surely we must be able to do something about this if we recognize it.

As I pondered this issue, I thought about born-again Christians, people whose lives completely lacked religion. Something or someone triggers something inside their minds that opens them to the wonder of God and Jesus Christ. It is as if someone let the genie out of the bottle; once it is out it is very difficult, if not impossible, to put back. Their belief, faith, and religion take over their lives. They read and study the Bible, go to prayer meetings, and change themselves and their lives.

I think perhaps that in the business world we see things superficially; we are not able to get that deeper understanding and meaning, that awareness of the greater purpose and interrelationship of influencing factors. It is interesting to see how psychotherapists and psychoanalysts have become so popular in the United States and how life coaches and mentors are becoming fashionable in Western society to help people understand their private and work lives. There is an increasing spiritual awareness driven by our need to make sense of our chaotic and complex business and private lives.

I think more people are recognizing the importance of self-understanding and, in particular, the intangible attributes we all hold and use to influence the successes in our lives. This is emotional intelligence, which is quite different from IQ. It relates to behaviors, relationships, and their affect on achievements. I think it is for professional psychologists and academics to get into the heart of these areas. But for us, the average business people, we need to gain only as much knowledge and understanding as is necessary for us to make sense of our lives and our situations.

Information overload is one of the greatest problems of our times. We live in the information age, information has never been more available, the Internet, satellite television, cable channels, tens of thousands of magazines and publications, and last but not least, e-mail. Added to that we have direct mail, telemarketing, advertising, text messaging, and spam. We are so connected in one way or another, it is unbelievable. If we get any more connected we will be plugging ourselves into computers before we go to bed. Virtual reality is beginning to merge with reality. There is as much misinformation as information. Is it any wonder we are all looking for answers? We all want and need to find the truth.

THE WAY AHEAD

I would like to think I could offer you a few alternatives. First, you can take this book at face value and use the knowledge and understanding it offers to add value to your business and private life. Second, you can join me on a continuing voyage of discovery and understanding designed to enable you to practically implement new knowledge and understanding in your personal and professional life.

Use this book as a reference tool for your own journey. I believe that, ultimately, it is up to you to design your map for the journey to business and personal success and self-understanding. You and your circumstances are different from those of other people. What is right for others might not be right for you. Your definition of success and achievement is probably very different from that of others.

Each reader will probably take away different things. If I were to summarize what I think are the most important points in this book, I would define them as follows. As you read them, bear in mind that I, too, am on a lifelong journey. As goals and aspirations change, I accept that my priorities may subsequently change. I hope you will do the same.

SUMMARY OF KEY CONCEPTS

- Most of the answers lie within you. You just need to find a way to release them.

- Success is a relative issue and different people will have different definitions.

- Gaining a better self-understanding is likely to make the greatest difference in your business and private lives.

- You have choices that enable you to make decisions that lead to actions that result in outcomes. These are your instruments of control. You can develop and enhance these to influence the outcomes you desire.

- Your business and private lives are different but intertwined. You should realize that you and your business are two different things.

- As a business leader, you have three roles: entrepreneur, manager, and worker. The attributes of each of these roles conflict with each other, and you must learn to balance them in your own circumstances.

- As a business leader you should work on your business, not in it.

- However big or small your business, you need to create a business model/machine driven by a documented system that can be used by people with the lowest possible level of skill to create consistency and quality above expectations in every aspect of the business.

- Business and life has become more complex. Threats are around every corner and the saying "survival of the fittest" can hardly be more relevant in today's environment. For every threat, however, there is a new opportunity. We can approach the future with an element of fear and trepidation or we can boldly look forward to exciting and profitable times.

- Your business and private life comprise a journey you can influence, but it is guaranteed to change.

- Developing and improving your emotional intelligence will enable you to change your behavior and increase your achievements.

- Allowing your subconscious mind to have influence can deliver great results.

CONTINUE THE VOYAGE TO BUSINESS AND PERSONAL SUCCESS WITH ASAP INSTITUTE AND JONATHAN BLAIN

Having read this far, you will have probably invested the nominal cover price of this book; at the very least you will have invested your time in thumbing through somebody else's copy. What concerns me is what value have you received for your investment? Has it been worth the time and effort? What difference is this book going to make to your private and business life? Has the book some entertainment value that helped you pass a long plane journey or kept you occupied while you waited for a train? Did it help alleviate the boredom of travel to and from work?

I am actually very interested in knowing. I would love to receive your thoughts and comments. Please feel free to contact me:

E-mail: jonathan.blain@asapinstitute.com

Please title your e-mail: Comments about your book, *The Business Voyage*.

PERSONAL DEVELOPMENT

ASAP Institute offers a number of bespoke products and services including:

❏ Personality Profile Report

❏ Self-Audit Questionnaire

❏ Entrepreneur Rating

❏ Managerial Rating

❏ Personal Action Plan Builder

❏ Personal Development Support Program

  • Executive Coach Scheme

  • Mentor Program

  • Personal Skills and Knowledge Development

   — Workshops

   — Seminars

   — Training Programs

BUSINESS DEVELOPMENT

❏ Business Blueprint Questionnaire

❏ Business Model/Business System

❏ Business Support Services

❏ Blue Water Visioning™ Program

❏ Customer Relationship Management Program

❏ Sales Management Program

❏ Technology Support Program

❏ ASAP Institute Business Academy Program

❏ Business Audit Services

❏ Business Plans

❏ Business Club

For sales enquiries email: **enquiry@asapinstitute.com** detailing your requirements.

REAL-LIFE STORY

Many years ago I met a New Zealander called Mike who was a boat builder by trade. He built his own yacht and set sail from New Zealand to sail around the World. Deep in the Southern Ocean, which is one of the remotest and most hostile places on earth, the winds are so strong that they are called the "roaring forties," "howling fifties" and the "screaming sixties." This reflects their latitudes and the strength of wind, and the waves can be a hundred feet tall or taller. In the middle of this isolation, Mike claims that God spoke to him and told him to go to the Falkland Islands and set up a christian mission for seamen.

Mike sold his yacht in Japan and moved to the east coast of the United Kingdom, where he bought an old wooden fishing boat that he renamed "King David." He thought it would be ideal for his mission. After buying the boat, he had little money to do it up and make it fit for the journey from the United Kingdom to the Falkland Islands. In the local Mission for Seamen, he met his wife and together they set about earning money to pay for equipment and materials. In their spare time evenings and weekends, they worked tirelessly on the boat. Their religion and faith ruled their lives. They joined the local Christian community and attended bible study classes. Mike worked on my own yacht, living in the boatyard on his boat. He lived the Christian life, he upheld the values of the Bible, and he never lost sight of his objective.

After nearly a year of very hard labor they were almost ready to depart, when disaster struck. Their boat was seriously damaged and the year of labor looked wasted. The local Christian community in Plymouth and the United Kingdom prayed for Mike and his family. By this time the couple had a young son. They also raised some money for the repairs and with great difficulty he succeeded in getting the boat ready. He could not afford fuel to motor his fishing boat to the Falkland Islands so he erected a large wooden mast with some sails. Against all the odds, he set sail and made the long and arduous journey with his young family to the hostile and unforgiving waters of the Falkland Islands. They weathered storms and fended off what they believed to be pirate attacks.

At the time, the Falkland Islands government had not given him permission for his mission, but he knew that this was his destiny, deemed by God, and eventually the Falkland Islanders welcomed him. There was something special about Mike. His belief, conviction, determination, passion, resilience, and his resolve would never falter with time. His determination never dwindled. He achieved his goal against all the odds.

I do not believe that Mike will ever lose his faith, religion, or appreciation of the Bible. I think he is likely to increase his knowledge, understanding, and commitment to them over time. What lessons can we learn from Mike's story?

INDEX

LEADERSHIP MASTER CLASS DVD SERIES
HELPING PEOPLE TO BECOME GREAT LEADERS
The World's Most Comprehensive DVD Series

Further details can be found on **www.leadershipmasterclass.org**

Jonathan Blain
Explorer, Innovator, Adventurer in Life and Business

AN AUTHORITY ON UNLOCKING HUMAN AND BUSINESS POTENTIAL

Available for:
- Keynote Presentations
- Consultancy
- Coaching
- Mentoring
- Non Executive Directorships

www.jonathanblain.com
jonathan.blain@jonathanblain.com
www.TheBusinessVoyage.com
www.LeadershipMasterclass.org
www.LeadersInLeadership.com
www.IDareToBeDifferent.org
www.SayNoToMediocrity.com
www.SayYesToExcellence.com
www.PeopleWhoChangeTheWorld.com

NEW BOOKS:

Call Me Now. Excellence in B2B Telephone Based Market Research, Lead Generation and Appointment Setting – How to get More for Less. (ISBN: 978-1-905243-04-4) www.CallMeNowBook.com

Packaged Solutions. (ISBN: 978-1-905243-03-7) www.PackagedSolutionsBook.com

The Low Cost Recruitment Revolution (ISBN: 978-1-905243-05-1) www.TheLowCostRecruitmentRevolution.com

KEYNOTE TALK

THE BUSINESS VOYAGE
SECRETS OF BUSINESS SUCCESS AND FULFILLMENT REVEALED
By Jonathan Blain, author

If you have enjoyed reading the book and have been inspired and motivated by its contents, why not invite Jonathan to do a keynote talk at your next event?

KEY AUDIENCE BENEFITS

See Differently — Become an Explorer

Develop curiosity ☆ Discover opportunity

Insight ☆ Meaning ☆ Purpose

Think Differently — Become an Innovator

Create new ideas ☆ Opportunity ☆ Leadership

Competitiveness ☆ Advantage

Act Differently — Become an Adventurer

Have the courage to commit and the determination to see
things through, whatever the consequences

Turn dreams into reality ☆ Embrace risk and uncertainty

Develop courage ☆ Achieve amazing things

Contact: www.jonathanblain.com keynote@jonathanblain.com

Printed in the United Kingdom
by Lightning Source UK Ltd.
114368UKS00001B/112-204